THE
PHENOMENOLOGICAL STUDY
OF THE
LOST GENERATION
OF
SUDAN

Elias Rinaldo Gamboriko, AJ. Ph.D

AuthorHouse™
1663 Liberty Drive
Bloomington, IN 47403
www.authorhouse.com
Phone: 1-800-839-8640

Published by AuthorHouse   01/13/2015

ISBN: 978-1-4969-6220-1 (sc)
ISBN: 978-1-4969-6219-5 (e)

Library of Congress Control Number: 2015900192

ABSTRACT

The purpose of this study is to examine the situation of the lost girls and boys of Sudan and to identify the effects caused by civil war in the country. The effects of war in the country left most Sudanese traumatized in refugee camps, while a few managed to relocate to the United States and settle in South Dakota. Through this study, some of the lived experiences of several lost girls and boys who have suffered psychologically and socially as a result of being exposed to civil war and being forced to relocate to the United States have been identified. The degree to which these Sudanese immigrants' current lives in the U.S. are affected by what they witnessed and experienced, as well as the extent to which their treatment was helpful in restoring their mental health, was also examined. Information from the interviews showed that each of the experiences of these young men and women were unique and that each immigrant coped with their experiences differently. One conclusion drawn from the study was that a majority of the support for these new immigrants should be given to those individuals who are 18 or older when they arrive.

ACKNOWLEDGEMENT

My sincere gratitude to my committee members, my chair Dr. Thomas Vail, Dr. Teresa Collins-Jones, for their support, guidance in the planning and implementation of this research project. I do appreciate the moral support rendered to me by all my classmates and the participants for their generous participation for the completion of this dissertation.

DEDICATION

To my parents, my confreres the Apostles of Jesus and friends. I would also like to thank the Adoration Sisters of the perpetual Adoration of the Blessed Sacrament for their prayers.

Contents

CHAPTER ONE

THE PROBLEM

Through both first-hand accounts and detailed statistical analyses, the story of the so-called "lost boys and girls" of Sudan demonstrates the ravaging effects of civil war on civilians and the extent to which these effects contribute to changing the lives of the victims in profound ways (Bixler, 2006; Bok, 2003; Dau, 2006; Dau & Akech, 2010; Eggers, 2006). In the wake of the second Sudanese civil war, which began in 1983, the foundations of statehood, personal livelihood, and the supporting survival mechanisms of the peoples of South Sudan "went up in flames," thus leaving the civilian population in dire servitude (Scroggins, 2004). Such occurrences followed hard on the heels of the first Sudanese civil war that lasted almost two decades, from 1955 until 1972 (Scroggins, 2004). A direct consequence of this civil war was that an entire generation of Sudanese was traumatized (Dau, 2006) immediately following similar experiences by their own parents and grandparents. The Sudanese civil war resulted in an enormous pool of civilian refugees who were displaced both within and outside the borders of their country, many of whom eventually found a new home in the United States and elsewhere (Fox & Willis, 2009; Luster, Qin, Bates, Johnson, & Rana, 2009; Luster et al., 2009; Magro, 2009).

Sudan hosts the largest population of displaced persons in the world and has produced one in every nine uprooted people in the world (Internal Displacement Monitoring Centre [IDMC], 2012). At the end of 1999, more than four million Sudanese were still displaced within the country and some 420,000 (IDMC, 2012) Sudanese refugees were living in neighboring countries (e.g., Uganda, Ethiopia, Kenya, Congo, Central African Republic, Chad, and Egypt). Since 1983, more than two million Sudanese have died as a direct result of the country's civil war, essentially amounting to one in every five of the entire Sudanese population according to some estimates (U.S. Committee for Refugees, 1999). An appreciation of the ensuing social context is needed in order to address the current research problem and the participants, namely the lost boys and girls of Sudan. The rationale for the term "lost" is the need to recognize both the high number of unaccompanied asylum-seeking adolescents among the Sudanese affected by the war and that fact that the majority of these adolescents will suffer from life-long after-effects that will inhibit them from leading a normal life (Hodes, Jagdev, Chandra, & Cunniff, 2008). As statistics from the United States Committee for Refugees (USCR, 1999) show, a clear indication exists that a high prevalence of psychological disorders similar to posttraumatic stress disorder (PTSD) persists among the members of the lost generation, thus raising legitimate concerns about their ability to lead optimum or normal lives.

On a clinical level, trauma involves the exposure to a physical or psychological threat or assault to a person's physical integrity, sense of self, safety, survival, or the physical safety of another significant individual in a person's life (American Psychiatric Association, 2000). The psychological results of trauma, which can be examined on a clinical level as a singular or ongoing experience (DePrince & Freyd, 2002), are likely to be associated with what is known as PTSD (Scurfield, 1985). PTSD is characterized by negative psychological arousal in patients who have experienced either singular or ongoing traumatic events such as assault, rape, war, or disasters (Scurfield, 2006). The foundation for identifying PTSD links to the early foundational psychoanalytic theories put forward by Freud (1956) that suggest that dysfunction and trauma are connected to the onset of dissociation and dissociative disorders.

At-risk for PTSD

According to Freud, one of the known pioneering scholars of stress-related psychological problems, "if a traumatic event had a magnitude of impact which overwhelmed coping resources, 'the mechanism of the ego,' including efforts to master the trauma in dream work might not succeed" (Freud, 1920/2012, p. 38). The foundation has given practitioners of psychological theory the ability to recognize trauma-related symptoms, an ability which has steadily continued to grow at a remarkable rate within the context of stress-related studies (Magro & Polyzoi, 2009). The ability to recognize symptoms has been particularly helpful for examining patients and developing treatments for the results of trauma (Scurfield, 1985). Many scientific studies demonstrated a connection between childhood stress, trauma, and coercion as the root cause (Anderson & Spencer, 2002; Beck, 1979; Beck, 1999; Beck, 1995). The connections have been accepted among the leading psychologists and other international experts with vested experience in the different stages of trauma.

Following exposure to a traumatic event, patients may re-experience the event(s), hallucinate, avoid situations or stimuli similar to the trauma (Schnurr et al., 2007), experience signs of depression and anxiety (Scurfield, 1985) and, as a result, find themselves socially and/or psychologically impaired (DePrince & Freyd, 2002). In chronic, traumatic situations, the environment where the trauma occurs almost always contains the implicit risk of danger, even in the absence of any actual trauma (Foa, Keane, & Friedman, 2000), which means that when people leave Sudan, it is more likely that they will begin to recover from their trauma. It is important to recognize that the signs and symptoms of PTSD can also look like different kinds of neuropsychiatric disorders, such as anger, aggression, dissociative disorders, and major depression (Frueh et al., 2009; Laufer, Brett, & Gallops, 1985).

Other challenges need to be managed in addition to the psychological symptoms of trauma. Physical reactions to trauma are not uncommon, and the costs for both the treatment of trauma and losses in productivity can be substantial for the patients, employers, and agencies that provide medical care (DePrince & Freyd, 2002). According to the *Diagnostic and Statistical Manual, Fourth Edition, Text Revision* (DSM-IV-TR), individuals tend to have fears and present disorganized behaviors, followed by three types of symptomatic forms of response for at least one month after witnessing a traumatic event (De Bellis, Hooper, Woolley, & Shenk, 2010). These responses can include: (a) the intrusive re-experiencing of the traumatic event(s); (b) persistent avoidance of stimuli associated with the traumatic events(s), including the numbing of emotional responses; and (c) persistent and increased physiological arousal (De Bellis et al., 2010, p. 570).

In order to diagnose a patient with PTSD, some or all of the above-mentioned signs and symptoms must be present for more than one month following the initial traumatic event, causing clinically significant disturbances in functioning (APA, 2000). A person is considered to have acute stress disorder when these criteria are met during the first month following a traumatic event. Such may include exposure to death or serious conflict. PTSD further characterizes as "acute" when present for less than three months, "chronic" when present for more than three months, or "delayed onset" when the initial symptoms develop approximately six months or more after the initial traumatic event (APA, 2000).

Although many options exist for the care and treatment of trauma survivors, it is also noted in the literature that, when looking at the situations of war survivors, little definitive understanding exists of the mechanisms and pathways involved in the simultaneous presence of depression and trauma. The literature indicated that the "co-morbidity of psychological symptoms is the result of a complex interaction of the number, nature, and duration of traumatic experiences along with demographic and developmental factors" (Morgos, Worden, & Gupta, 2008, p. 231). The lack of definitive understanding means that the diagnosis of trauma is inevitably more complex for the survivors of war or civil conflicts, such as those who survived the conflicts in Sudan (Jones, 2004). Rahim, Abdelmonium, and Anwar (2009) noted that the majority of Sudan survivors are children. Considering that their physical displacement occurred during a critical time in their development and that, during displacement, many have been exposed to physical or sexual violence, it is not surprising that the Sudanese children who have been diagnosed with trauma and depression are also affected by a number of physiological disorders. These disorders further complicate their treatment for trauma (Rahim et al., 2009).

Various studies performed over the last several years that were designed to study the occurrence of trauma within the Sudanese population of refugees have led to the development of epidemiological and theoretical aspects of trauma associated with abuse, violence, and coercion (Dau, 2006; USCR, 2000). According to Bixler (2006), the children who are the "lost generation of Sudan" have gone through a very tumultuous childhood that ultimately resulted in the sacrifice of their psychosocial wellbeing. Moreover, prior to immigrating to the United States, approximately 80% of the lost generation of Sudan spent, on average, 14 years within various refugee camps that momentarily provided safe shelter (Bixler, 2006, p. 18). These aspects of psychopathology interfere with the everyday lives of these patients and their abilities to function normally, as mentioned above (Jones, 2004).

Statement of the Problem

Being at-risk for PTSD is a major challenge facing the lost generation of Sudanese children. The immense devastation during the Sudanese civil war and the resulting trauma to which this generation was exposed left them vulnerable to psychological disorders. The generation witnessed of the burning of their homes, displacement, hunger, death, and participation in combat at a tender age, thus being traumatized. The combined effects of the war traumas suffered during the Sudanese conflict resulted in a number of psychological disorders arising among the children of this generation. Currently, the stories of this Sudanese generation are not being told despite the fact that the impacted individuals require immediate and effective help. The forms of psychological trauma suffered by this generation need to be understood and integrated into careful diagnosis of trauma to ensure that this specific and large generation of war survivors can be effectively treated on long term. Past studies have failed to address the issues related to such disorders, being inclined instead to concentrate on other matters such as the economic challenges faced by the Sudanese people following the war, the number of refugees in various locations, and the causes of the Sudanese struggle. In an effort to understand the effects on this lost generation of Sudanese children, whose lives and psychological security suffered damage due to living in such dangerous environments, this study used a phenomenological approach, effective in assessing trauma (Jones, 2004).

Purpose of the Study

The purpose of this study was to explore the lived experiences of the lost boys and girls and present their experiences through phenomenological research, thus allowing their stories to provide an understanding of the nature and effect of the experience of being a Sudanese refugee relocated in the United States (Magro & Polyzoi, 2009). Through this research, an attempt was made to establish the psychological connections between the traumatic experiences of the lost generation of Sudan and the eventual development of trauma. It is undeniable that the lost generation of Sudan, because of their past traumatic experiences, requires effective psychological and spiritual intervention.

Research Question

What are the lived experiences of the lost boys and girls of Sudan who currently live in the United States?

Definitions of Terms

The following are the definitions of the terms used in this study and the foundations for their scholarly use.

Acute Stress Disorder. According to the *Diagnostic and Statistical Manual, Fourth Edition, Text Revision* (DSM-IV-TR, 2000), this is a form of posttraumatic stress disorder (PTSD) that is diagnosed when the criteria for the disorder are met during the first month following a traumatic event. This form of trauma is further characterized as "acute" when present for less than three months, "chronic" when present for more than three months, and "delayed onset" when the initial symptoms develop approximately six months or more after the initial traumatic event (DSM-IV-TR, 2000).

Displacement. This occurs when civilian refugees are displaced from their homes, either within or outside the borders of a country, after or during a conflict (Fox & Willis, 2009).

Lost boys and girls of Sudan. These are the unaccompanied, asylum-seeking children and adolescents who have been affected by the Sudanese civil war and have been psychologically and often physically affected by the traumatic events they experienced (Hodes et al., 2008).

Posttraumatic Stress Disorder (PTSD). PTSD is a recurring psychological arousal that occurs in patients after experiencing singular or repeated traumatic events such as assault, rape, war, or disasters (Scurfield, 2006).

Trauma. This term can be categorized as exposure to either a physical or psychological threat or assault to a person's physical integrity, sense of self, safety, and/or survival, or to the physical safety of another significant individual in a person's life (DSM-IV-TR, 2000). The signs and symptoms of PTSD can mimic various neuropsychiatric disorders, including anger, aggression, dissociative disorders, and major depression (Frueh et al., 2009; Laufer et al., 1985).

Limitations of the Study

The limitations of the study include the following:

1. Because this study was limited to one location involving participants displaced from the Sudan to the U.S. particularly, the findings cannot represent the entire study population (i.e. Sudan refugees in all regions worldwide). The study assumed that the results generated from the U.S. refugees (i.e. the sample) would be a representation of the entire refugee population across the globe.

2. Because this was a phenomenological study, it focused on individual experiences rather than empirical data.

3. This investigation was limited to one instrument, the interview, further described in the Appendix. The limitation to one data-collection instrument implies that there may be factors not captured in the study.

4. The study acknowledges that there are factors other than those listed here that could also influence the psychological recovery and development of the lost boys and girls of Sudan. Some of these factors include a safe environment, food security, and education and a belief system.

5. Delimitations of the Study

   The delimitations of the study include the following:

   1. The study did not include an analysis of any demographic data or its potential linkage to the experiences or outcomes of the participants' phenomenological reports or their identified qualities. Although these factors may have had an effect on the experiences of the participants, personal data has been determined to be outside the bounds of this study because of the potentially complex arguments that could be linked back to participants' psychological recovery and development.

   2. All data on Sudan and its conflict(s) included in this study were limited to what is available in the public domain, and no additional information was collected for the purposes of this study.

Significance of the Study

Over the last few years, a number of researchers have taken a special interest in documenting the stories detailing the agonies of children who had to endure the ravages of the civil war in Sudan as they escaped to seek refuge in neighboring countries such as Kenya, Uganda, and Ethiopia (Bixler, 2006; Bok, 2004; Dau, 2006; Eggers, 2006). Details of the struggles that Sudanese children had to endure are documented by personal narrative accounts that tell the stories of how families and entire neighborhoods were destroyed, the treacherous journeys to refugee camps, and of course, the difficulties encountered in these various refugee camps. All these experiences were most likely extremely stressful. According to Natsios (2008), the problem is nevertheless becoming larger than the Sudanese context alone:

[O]ver the past half-century civil war has replaced international war as the most prevalent form of large-scale violence. Once started, civil wars are hard to stop: they persist for more than ten times as long as international wars. Their consequences are usually dire, being massively destructive to the economy, to the society, and to life itself. (p. 2)

This statement indicates that there is a need to develop a more comprehensive psychosocial response to the types of conflict and violence facing these young people today.

Given that this problem could potentially grow over the next few years and that millions of Sudanese young people are likely to face trauma-related mental health challenges, an immediate need exists for new research on the needs of the lost generation of Sudan. As noted by Morgos et al. (2008), a recent study of Sudanese youth indicated that "[75%] of the children met the DSM-IV criteria for PTSD, and 38% exhibited clinical symptoms of depression. The percentage of children endorsing significant levels of grief symptoms was 20%" (p. 229). Research in the area of traumas suffered by Sudanese people, therefore, lead to the development of new psychological support methods for young people affected by civil war conflicts on a broader scale (Magro & Polyzoi, 2009).

Overview of the Study

The research methodology for this project is a qualitative case study approach that used a phenomenological framework for interacting with the participants, namely those identified as the lost boys and girls of Sudan. The research project is a qualitative design that is consistent with Moustakas's (1994) transcendental phenomenological research method. Moustakas's (1994) approach, which redefines the traditional role of subjects in qualitative research, uses rigorous systematic procedures and a detailed methodology (Moerer-Urdahl & Creswell, 2004). As cited in Moerer-Urdahl and Creswell (2004), the qualitative framework for phenomenological studies is characterized by participants sharing commonalities related to experiencing the same phenomenon.

The primary data collection tool for this study was a qualitative interview developed specifically for this study. The interviews consisted of open-ended questions and integrated yes/no questions when appropriate. Up to 18 questions were asked at the beginning of the interviews, depending on what was needed to allow each of the Sudanese refugees to come forward with their ideas and experiences.

A purposive sampling method was used in this study; specifically, the stakeholder approach for purposive sampling was used, whereby individuals (selected from the known population of Sudanese refugees in the United States) who have the most to benefit from the analysis of this research topic were utilized for this study (Babbie & Benaquisto, 2002). Moustakas (1994) reported that no preconditions exist for identifying and selecting research participants within this phenomenological research model. Moustakas (1994) also stated, however, that research participants must have experienced the phenomenon and be willing to participate. A significant percentage of the individuals in the lost generation who participated in this research were from peasant backgrounds in South Sudan who have relocated to the United States. They are mainly from communities and settlements around Juba, Aweil, and Wau and are predominantly from the Dinka tribe (Magro & Polyzoi, 2009).

CHAPTER TWO

REVIEW OF THE LITERATURE

According to Wild, Wild, and Han (2008), globalization can increase wealth and efficiency in developed and developing nations, thereby creating jobs and decreasing poverty. The trend toward greater economic, cultural, political, and technological interdependence among national institutions and economies, according to the findings of Wild et al. (2008), is a process that ensures that the smallest nations will be able to maximize the uses of their resources and improve the standard of living of their inhabitants. For this reason, many African nations, once considered insignificant players in the global economy, are now being targeted because of their extensive growth. Following the discovery of world-class oil reserves in Sudan, the country was identified as one of these key players (Kramer, 1996). At the same time, because of inflation, high population growth, and the external control of these oil reserves, the real growth of the gross domestic product (GDP) of Sudan has not changed significantly over the last 20 years(Okumu & Ikelegbe, 2010). In addition, food security and other economic issues have caused ongoing stress on the population (Keen & Lee, 2006). Such economic issues and the continuous stress have resulted in an ongoing conflict that has escalated into a longstanding civil war characterized by extensive violence. This is the backdrop against which the lost boys and girls of Sudan have been made to fend for themselves (Marlowe, 2010).

The literature review examines the different factors that have led to these challenges throughout the recent history of Sudan, most specifically in the Darfur region. The literature on the nature of the Sudanese conflict was examined in order to identify the ways in which individuals in this area of the world have been affected by the stress of living in a conflict zone (Marlowe, 2010). In addition, the specific challenges faced by refugees are explored, as well as the ways in which psychological distress such as PTSD and acute stress disorder affect refugees. The literature review takes into consideration the literature on this study's chosen methodology, namely that of phenomenology, and the ways in which this study complements existing scholarly research. Finally, the literature review ends with a summary of these findings.

Historical Context of the Sudanese Conflict

The idea of economic development is fraught with challenges, both practical and ideological. As Isbister (2008) suggested, the fact that countries with significant financial and social resources act to assist those who do not have these resources may demonstrate a different form of colonialism that funds the social behaviors and administrative decisions that fit into a very narrow view of what it means to be "developed." As Todaro and Smith (2009) wrote, "at the dawn of the industrial era, real living standards in the richest countries were no more than three times as great as those of the poorest. Today the ratio approaches 110 to 1" (p. 78). Neocolonialism, therefore, could be considered the deliverance of structural changes in foreign lands that serve its own purposes, thereby increasing production mechanisms within developing countries, such as Sudan, so that goods, and now services, can be inexpensively produced.

The challenge is that the populations of countries such as Sudan often suffer for the sake of economic gain. Looking at the bigger picture, for the last several decades, transnational institutions such as the World Bank, the International Monetary Fund, and several United Nations agencies have suggested that deregulation and privatization will lead to economic development in the world's poorest nations. As Handleman (2008) wrote, however, "while some Third World [countries] are underdeveloped in all major aspects of modernization, others are far more advanced" (p. 3). Nevertheless, because knowledge is in many ways akin to power and codified by neocolonial actions, those who impose these terms on the world believe that they are doing the right thing. As Easterly (in Griffiths, 2010) noted, "the 'one correct answer' came to mean 'free markets,' and, for the poor world, it was defined as doing whatever the IMF and the World Bank tell you to do" (p. 12). These experts believe that structural changes can be made to balance the economic playing field and allow countries with the lowest rates of economic growth to catch up to the rates of expansion seen in countries such as China and India. These countries have demonstrated the ability to erase some of the devastating poverty they faced in the previous century (Marlowe, 2010).

How has this approach to global development affected Sudan? As Marchal (2008) noted, the conflict in Sudan has always been an international one, linked not only to the challenge of managing resources (a challenge faced by many other African nations such as Chad and Eritrea), but also to challenges linked to the Middle East as well. As Marchal (2008) notes:

> [T]he international perception of events in the region continues to be a prisoner of the colonial order: Sudan and Darfur are indeed linked to the United Kingdom and the Anglo-Saxon world, while Chad inherits a French touch, Arab tribes settled in Darfur and became part of the conflict that broke out there after the devastating drought in 1984. (p. 430)

In other words, the legacy of colonialism and the drive for power over Sudan's significant resources became the framework for what was to become a devastating conflict between members of many different nations, even though the bulk of the conflict has taken place within the borders of Sudan.

This range of political actors in Sudan also means that there is the involvement of a variety of ethnic groups as well, which has increased pressure on the potential for conflict. The people of this region of Africa are diverse in that they represent dozens of language divisions, tribes, and ideologies. At the same time, the people of this region are commonly affected by the hegemonic powers brought to their region by multinational companies as a legacy of colonialism. As noted by Kramer (1996), Turkish and Mahdist regimes have been involved in Sudan since the 19th century, resulting in the introduction of Shari'a law in September 1983. Nonetheless, a significant proportion of the country's population is Christian or animist of African, rather than Islamic, descent. The confluence of religious views results in "the bifurcation of Sudan between Northern/Arab/Islamic and Southern/animist-Christian which presupposes 'a degree of racial, cultural, and religious homogeneity that oversimplifies and falsifies a dynamic picture of pluralism with internal differences'" (Kramer, 1996, p. 142). Therefore, the bifurcation means that the foundation of this country has been forged by the lack of acceptance of the diversity that inherently exists in the community.

On a political level, similar challenges can be found. Kramer (1996) wrote that Sudan has been faced with

> the deterioration of coalition politics into "a game of musical chairs"; corrupt and incompetent administration, leading to a foreign debt that by 1985 exceeded the country's GDP; and the unwillingness and/or inability of northern politicians to endorse the good intentions of the Koka Dam agreement (1986), leaving intact the "September Laws" that have fueled civil war. (p. 141)

In addition, Wassara (cited in Okumu & Ikelegbe, 2010) stated the following:

> The present Sudan is the product of the Turko-Egyptian military campaigns in search of gold and slaves led by Mohamed Ali from Egypt in 1821. The expansion of the invasion into the Blue Nile, the Nuba Mountains, and later to the southern part of Sudan brought together populations with different origins. . . . The slave trade during the Turko-Egyptian period and the Mahdist regime at the end of the 19th century left its mark on ethnic relationships in Sudan. Reference to native Sudanese by some northerners as slaves perpetuates distrust and indignation. These ancient hatreds revive identity differentiations and violent rivalries, contributing to prolonged conflict in Sudan. (p. 266)

This history means that a number of salient forces have pushed the population of Sudan into extreme stress and discontent with its current state of affairs. The result is that Sudan's population has been fractured into hundreds of Sudanese rebel groups, which are organized, armed movements that have risen up against the central government in Khartoum in order to pursue identity, nationalism, justice, political rights, and change (Wassara, as cited in Okumu & Ikelegbe, 2010, p. 22). These rebel groups have organized specific campaigns against each other and against the government since the 1950s. Some of these rebel groups, such as the Sudan People's Liberation Army (SPLA), which is an African group, have taken on more of a peacekeeping role in recent years. Other groups, such as the Sudan Liberation Movement/Army (SLM/A), an Islamic group, have been fractured into subgroups as peace talks have broken down (Wassara, as cited in Okumu & Ikelegbe, 2010, p. 275). The result has been increased factionalism, which has led to development of new African tribal rebel groups that respond to the violence of the SLM/A and their associates. McEvoy and LeBrun (2010) noted that the factionalism has led to massacre upon massacre as both tribal and religious groups fight each other, resulting in the deaths of two million people over the course of the past 20 years.

In addition to these factions, a government-led group called the Janjaweed militia group became one of the leading forces of violence after the Darfur rebellion in 2003. This group has been described as "an 'Arab' paramilitary militia group on camels and horses and is known for perpetrating violence against civilians in Darfur" (Wassara, as cited in Okumu & Ikelegbe, 2010, p. 277). In other words, as the conflict escalated, the government of Sudan began to take extreme measures against non-rebel citizens as a way to control their movements and ideologies. The attacks by the Janjaweed were also meant to affect the economic and racial control of the country, which is why, in part, the popularity of the rebel forces in the region increased after 2003 (Wassara, in Okumu & Ikelegbe, 2010, p. 279). As noted by McEvoy and LeBrun (2010), the popularity of rebel groups has created a Sudanese culture that is deeply connected to the use of extreme military force in every situation, and the use of small arms abounds, even after the 2011 split between Sudan and the newly formed Republic of South Sudan. This means that, even as the tides change in this region, continued atrocities have been forced upon the nonmilitant populations of Sudan and South Sudan.

Experiences of Sudanese Refugees

The number of Sudanese refugees is almost countless. Roberts, Damundu, Lomoro, and Sondorp (2009) noted:

> [U]p to four million people were forcibly displaced from their homes as internally displaced persons (IDPs) and they went mainly to Khartoum in the north, central Sudan, or the towns of Southern Sudan. There were also up to one million refugees, living mainly in camps and cities in Kenya, Uganda, Central Africa Republic, Ethiopia, Egypt, and other neighboring countries. (p. 245)

These statistics and observations were all made prior to 2005. The amount is more than quadruple the number of refugees from either Rwanda or Afghanistan at the heights of their respective conflicts (Salehyan, 2008). Nevertheless, displacement still continues today, and the ways in which refugees are displaced and were displaced is also hard to ascertain. McEvoy and LeBrun (2010) provided details on the conflict's refugees for the last year on record, 2009, as shown in Table 1.

Table 1:
Notable violent clashes that targeted women & children in 2009 (McEvoy & LeBrun, 2010, p. 7)

Month	Location	State	Wounded	Killed	Displace
March	Lekwongole	Jonglei	45	450	5000
April	Akobo	Jonglei	70	250	15,000
May	Torkej	Upper Nile	57	71	10,000
June	Nyaram	Upper Nile	38	60	10,000
August	Mareng	Jonglei	18	185	n/a

August	Panyangor	Jonglei	64	42	24,000
September	Duk Padiet	Jonglei	100	160	n/a
October	Terekeka	Central Equatoria	n/a	30	22000
Totals			**392+**	**1,248**	**86,000+**

Table 1 demonstrates that even after a peace accord was put into place, thousands of individuals were still being displaced in Sudan on an ongoing basis. As noted by Pantuliano and Elhawary (2009), this displacement occurred because "post conflict transitions are often accompanied by continued violence, at times culminating in a resumption of war. Countries may suddenly find peace, but competition over land may continue and may regress into conflict" (p. 2). In addition, as noted by Sorbo (2010), part of the reason for the ongoing conflict and the need to escape is the itinerant nature of some of the cultures in Sudan. Sorbo (2010) wrote that Sudan has the highest concentration of traditional pastoralists in the world, and food security and economic issues result in different pastoralist groups and farmers using the political conflict as a means to justify their own violence against one another. In other words, even if there is an agreement that a conflict should end, there is also a need to recognize that the social forces behind a conflict will not necessarily go away (Giorgi, 2006).

The challenge, according to Salehyan (2008), is that the appearance of refugees can obviously strain the relationships that exist between the countries that produce conflict survivors and the countries that take them in. In the case of Sudan, refugees ended up in a number of neighboring countries, such as Chad, Kenya, and Uganda, but they also ended up in places further away with more resources, such as Ghana, the European Union, and the United States. Edwards (2008) wrote that the continuing problems in Sudan would only continue to escalate as the migration cycles of traditionally nomadic and pastoral communities grow larger as climate change takes effect. People will be forced to go further and further abroad in order to maintain food security (Keen & Lee, 2006). In addition, according to Shanmugaratnam (2008):

> [P]ast experience has shown that multinationals and some foreign governments such as that of China had no compunction about collaborating with the Sudanese government which adopted violent means to evict people to clear land for oil extraction and used the oil revenue to intensify the wars in the south and other parts of the country. (p. 9)

This suggests that, as Sudan becomes more economically challenged, there is the potential for these types of refugee movements to continue.

Behavior changes have been evident among the Sudan refugees, especially among the children, who have limited capacity of controlling their emotional responses towards such changes. As noted by Jordans, Komproe, Tol, and De Jong (2009), the overall symptoms of psychosocial distress, which are prevalent among war-affected children from Sudan, include social withdrawal, aggression, hyperactivity, and dominating behaviors. Jordans et al. (2009) also noted that the majority of the young Sudanese refugees that they studied are older, on average, than refugees from other countries and came mainly from rural areas prior to moving to refugee camps, either internal or external to Sudan. Srinivasa Murthy (2008) noted there are other demographic variables specific to the experiences of refugees in the Sudan conflict. From an operational perspective, women are more likely to be affected by trauma than men, as are children and the elderly (Marlowe, 2010).

Nevertheless, as noted by Srinivasa Murthy (2008), there is a barrier to psychosocial-based community intervention within refugee camps because mental disorders are often seen as deviant under the social structure of this region, especially in the northern part of the country. The barrier means that it is unlikely, even in the best-case scenarios where people are provided with security and food, that they will be treated for stress-related disorders in these camps. Part of the challenge, as noted by Abdelnour et al. (2008), is that the focus of refugee camps has always been on immediate survival, and even that is hard to realize over the short term because of the inability to deliver food to the rural regions of Sudan and neighboring countries. Abdelnour et al. (2008) wrote:

> The majority of food in the camps is received though aid. Internally displaced persons (i.e. IDPs) stated that the food aid received is not sufficient and that they require more and different types of food. There is a need for market-based food distribution in the camps and this need will only increase when relief efforts decrease and agriculture and livestock-related enterprise can be effectively developed. (p. 70)

Providing food aid, however, is next to impossible over the short- to mid-term, as noted by Abdelnour et al. (2008), because it can take years for a refugee community to be placed and managed, especially when conflicts are ongoing.

PTSD and Acute Stress Disorder

For those individuals who do find their way out of refugee camps, they will face additional challenges as they work to recover on a psychological level. As noted in Chapter One, trauma can be categorized as exposure to a physical or psychological threat or assault to a person's physical integrity, sense of self, safety, survival, or the physical safety of another significant individual in a person's life (DSM-IV, 2000). The results of trauma, which can be categorized as singular or ongoing experiences (DePrince & Freyd, 2002) are likely to be associated with what is known as PTSD (Scurfield, 1985). A person is diagnosed with acute stress disorder when these criteria are met during the first month following a traumatic event, such as a combat-based disaster. PTSD is further characterized as "acute" when the symptoms are present for less than three months, "chronic" when symptoms are present for more than three months, or "delayed onset" when the initial symptoms develop approximately six months or more after the initial traumatic event (DSM-IV, 2000).

The intergenerational and spousal transmission of interpersonal violence, such as physical assault, or exposure to domestic violence, such as rape, which were common in the Sudanese conflict, are likely to have been experienced by trauma sufferers (Dixon, Browne, & Hamilton-Giachritsis, 2005). These experiences have lasting effects on their long-term relationships throughout their lives. In addition, with respect to the onset of trauma, Schechter, Zygmunt, Coates, Davies, and Trabka (2007) noted that parents' experiences with social violence and the severity of their own violence-related trauma symptoms could be used to predict accurately specific trauma challenges among their children. The challenges include (a) deregulated aggression and aggression, (b) intentional bias to danger and distress, and (c) avoidance of and withdrawal from conflicts (p. 187). Addressing trauma sometimes requires treatment and counseling of the whole family, rather than just the affected individuals.

In addition, loss of sleep or chronic sleep deprivation, both of which are common in conflict situations, can produce direct effects on the functions of the prefrontal cortex, affecting both cognitive performance and the speed at which responses to minor psychomotor tasks are made (Wesensten & Belenky, 2005). Sleep deprivation also negatively affects complex cognitive processes, such as being able to judge, anticipate, form, and implement a plan of action, and maintain situational awareness and carry out critical reasoning processes (Wesensten & Belenky, 2005). Such matters could be managed by instituting a number of measures that will help in addressing the underlying issues. According to Wesensten and Belenky (2005), six essential components must be incorporated into an action plan. The two most crucial elements are collaborative and situational understanding of the individual's personal situation. However, these components are ineffective unless the necessary resources, such as patient training in recognizing the inciting events and symptoms, are provided. In addition, it is essential to understand the contribution of intermediate factors such as sleep deprivation. If an individual's operational capacities can be predicted, then his or her stress levels and cognitive performance can also be predicted (Wesensten & Belenky, 2005).

Few randomized controlled trials have been conducted on the use of psychopharmacological agents to treat patients exposed to traumatic events, so more studies are needed to determine whether these might be effective treatments over the long term (De Roos, Greenwald, de Jongh, & Noorthoorn, 2004). Both CBT and Eye-Movement Desensitization and Reprocessing (EMDR) have been shown to lower stress-related symptoms in individuals with trauma significantly in clinical settings, with EMDR reported as slightly more effective in some instances (De Roos et al., 2004). Additional treatments, such as narrative-, massage-, and art-based therapies for survivors of conflict, have also been proposed and explored in small studies, but none have been extensively studied using long-term studies with strict study protocols (Van-Der, 1996).

The types of PTSD that are known to affect children can be traced back to studies performed by Beck (1979, 1999). Beck (1995) watched his patients and became interested in how they patients viewed and "communicated" with themselves. These observations led Beck to believe that his patients had already formed their own sets of beliefs. Based on the belief his patients had already formulated their own thought patterns, which he would later label "schemas," Beck (1979) theorized that his patients' schemas set the pattern of how they perceived their experiences to external stimuli and, as such, his patients' schemas would dictate how the patients would view their experiences and respond to external stimuli. Beck (1979) further recognized that what his patients believed did not always match what he thought was a deeper understanding of the issues at hand. From the findings, Beck (1979) theorized that his patients' worldview was often distorted by their own internal dialogues and schemas. Beck then expanded on his theories and said that if he could change his patients' schemas, he could change the way his patients viewed their experiences. The change in patient view, in turn, could lead to changes in their maladaptive behaviors (Beck, 1995).

According to Beck (1979), an individual's core beliefs begin to take shape in childhood, and these beliefs are reinforced and developed into semi-permanent schemas. Normal childhood development often includes occasional negative thoughts about oneself but, usually, a well-developed child will believe he or she is likable (Beck, 2005). However, if the child continues to experience negative feelings or, more appropriately, if the child perceives that his or her experiences are negative because of the traumatic events he or she has experienced, then the child may attribute the negative feelings to himself or herself. Giorgi (2006) observed that the occurrence is especially true because children, in general, tend to view the adults in their lives as more experienced and less likely to make mistakes (Beck, 2005). Negative core beliefs may be turned into solidified negative schemas through which the child will then filter all incoming information, thus distorting the very nature and understanding of how the child perceives himself or herself. The eventual culmination of this cycle is that the stimuli support a dysfunctional core belief system (Beck, 1979; Beck, 2005). The existence of a dysfunctional core belief system explains why children who have emerged from the Sudanese conflict are often afflicted with social withdrawal, aggression, hyperactivity, and dominating behaviors (Van Manen, 2007).

Beck (1999) noted that children tend to over-generalize "other's unpleasant actions" (p.8) within their own families and utilize "hostile framing" (p.8) as a consequence of their overgeneralization, thus leading to the formation of distorted cognitions and beliefs. A "negative cognitive shift" occurs when individuals focus on negative information or thought patterns instead of focusing on positive information or thought patterns (Beck, 1979). According to Beck, a negative cognitive shift occurs when individuals distort observations or cognitive events, resulting in the over-exaggeration of the negative aspects of these events. Individuals will then, at times, see things as black and white and continue to over-generalize these events (Giorgi, 2006). The individual then reinforces these negative distortions by saying things such as "I can never do things right" or "my life is hopeless" Beck, 1979). Beck (1999) further suggests that such thinking can become automatic in individuals, resulting in the rapid development of negative schemas, especially after repeated exposure to traumatic events. Over time, such a form of thinking can lead to the solidification of this core belief and a new schema will appear, albeit a negative one.

Beck further theorized that there is rarely a single causal factor for most psychological disorders. He stated that people who suffer from psychological distress have most likely been exposed to many environmental, biological, and social challenges. Beck (1999) states that the effect is especially true in children because they often lack the necessary experience or training to understand the different environmental factors that cause their psychological distress. Beck also indicated that children often have difficulty making realistic goals and often make incorrect assumptions, both of which can lead to distorted thinking patterns. Because children have less experience to draw from, they tend to think and act irrationally when facing a threatening situation (Beck, 1999).

Beck (1979) wrote extensively about "automatic thoughts" and indicated that these automatic thoughts play a crucial role in the cognitive processing of "perceived" distress in children. Beck (1979, 1999) believed that psychological distress does not stem from inaccurate thoughts, but rather distress most likely stems from the combination of biological, environmental, and social factors.

In the case of Sudanese refugees, Roberts, Damundu, Lomoro, and Sondorp (2010) noted that demographic components often determine if these biological, environmental, and social factors lead to the onset of full-blown trauma. As an example, they noted that access to soap and clean water often has a psychologically beneficial effect on children growing up in conflict. For those able to access soap and water, there was the calming effect of being able to control their own environment; those without access experienced higher levels of anxiety. Roberts et al. (2009) also noted that certain experiences, such as avoiding rape, help Sudanese survivors cope and avoid trauma.

Methodological Literature on Phenomenology

This study used a phenomenological qualitative research framework, which can be traced back to Husserl's (1931) phenomenological and theoretical explanation of internal psychological research analysis. Husserl (1931) suggested that the internal experiences of one group cannot be analyzed and the findings applied to another group with very different experiences. Therefore, based on Husserl's line of thinking and the current research conditions, research conclusions and recommendations that are based on the viewpoint of individuals who have not personally experienced life as a refugee in a conflict zone should not be the basis for policies and theoretical development of people who have been affected by conflict. Perhaps the hostility and fear directed at people who have been refugees generates from developing unreliable policies and theoretical frameworks that largely rely on the inherent negative viewpoints of non-refugee individuals who have not suffered from trauma or any other stress-related ailment.

Likewise, Snygg (1941) reached the same conclusion when he cautioned that predictions about one group's experiences could not be based upon conclusions obtained from scientific inquiry and research based on the previous observations and inner experiences of a different group. Snygg (1941) declared that, because of this type of methodology, psychological research theory has become defective. The failure of research efforts to describe the real-life experiences of the lost boys and girls of Sudan indicates the lack of understanding regarding the importance of what Rosenthal (1991) described as the biological activity of the human organism, which is the foundation of meaning and knowledge.

Heidegger (1962, 1967), Sartre (1967), Merleau-Ponty (1945/1962), Van Manen (1990), and Brentano (1874/2009) have all had a profound impact on the constructs used in phenomenology. Merleau-Ponty (1945/1962) described phenomenological research as a method that can be used to evaluate an individual's viewpoint about their experiences as they occur. Therefore, this science-based research methodology had been available for at least 60 years prior to Ponterotto's (2005) expressed concerns about the relevancy of psychological research. In addition, Snygg's (1941) early work emphasized that psychological research studies should be constructed from the viewpoint of the organism's behavior. Van Manen (1990) also described the need for psychological studies to have direct contact with real-world experiences. Snygg's (1941)viewpoint is exemplified by Leedy and Ormrod (2005), who explained that people involved in phenomenological studies are able to describe perspectives in terms of how they were personally influenced by specific phenomena. Additionally, Moustakas (1994) reported that the phenomenological approach involves finding the meaning and essence of an experience by listening to each participant describe his or her own experiences.

Similarly, Creswell (2007) concluded that phenomenological studies are able to describe the experiences of a concept or phenomena as it affects an individual. Creswell (2007) also reported that the qualitative framework of phenomenological studies is characterized by participants sharing the same experiences associated with the phenomenon. These studies underscored the importance of how the phenomenological approach is relevant to the study of children who have experienced traumatic events over an extended period. Moustakas' (1994) transcendental phenomenological research method appears to be the most appropriate choice for uncovering the hidden meaning of the lived experiences of the lost girls and boys of Sudan.

How the Current Study Enhances the Literature

That aim of this study was to demonstrate the need to recognize that the lost generation of Sudan has gone through a very tumultuous childhood that ultimately resulted in the sacrifice of their psychosocial wellbeing (Van Manen, 2007). The sacrifice has been caused by deep and profound social issues that are broader than the simple experience of acute stress or trauma. The survivors of the Sudanese conflict, who were children at the time they were exposed to war, are likely to have been immersed in a way of life that suggested to them that violence is one of the only ways to respond to challenges.

Using a phenomenological approach, this study utilized the narratives provided by the survivors of the Sudanese conflict to look at the manner in which the lived experiences of the lost generation of Sudan affected their current lives in the US.

CHAPTER THREE

METHODOLOGY

The purpose of this study was to explore the lived experiences of the lost boys and girls of Sudan and to present their experiences through phenomenological research, thus allowing their stories to provide an understanding of the nature and effect of what it is like to be a child soldier. This chapter provides details on the research design, the method that was followed in conducting the research (i.e. qualitative) plus the relevant information on the target population and sample group that was studied using this methodology. This chapter describes the ways in which the qualitative phenomenological technique was used and its importance as a framework for the present study. A phenomenological study is one in which an exploration is performed whereby multifaceted and meaningful data can be mined, resulting in the development of clear conclusions (Anderson & Spenser, 2002).

Description of the Research Design

The methodology for this study was a qualitative case study approach that used a phenomenological framework for interacting with the study participants, namely those identified as the lost boys and girls of Sudan. The research project used a qualitative design that is consistent with the transcendental phenomenological research method described by Moustakas (1994). Moustakas' (1994) approach, which redefined the traditional role of subjects in qualitative research, uses rigorous systematic procedures and a detailed methodology (Moerer-Urdahl & Creswell, 2004). Creswell (2006) also characterized the qualitative framework of a phenomenological study as one where participants share similar experiences that are all associated with a given phenomenon.

Githens (2007) explains that immersing oneself in the experiences described during in-depth interviews allows the researcher to experience the phenomenon being studied. Such an approach provides the researcher with the ability to not only identify, but also to explore and fully understand the phenomenological experiences rather than specifically relying on external explanations of the research findings. Such an approach also provides a mechanism for the researcher to gain unique perspective, insight, and understanding of the situation rather than relying on external statistics to infer reason (Karami, Ahmadi, & Reshadatjoo, 2006).

Instruments

The primary instrument used in this study was qualitative interviews, which was created exclusively for this research process. The interviews used the open-ended questions, as well as yes/no questions where appropriate. Up to 18 questions were asked to begin the conversation, depending on what was needed to allow each Sudanese refugee to come forward with their ideas and experiences (Pizarro, 2010). Qualitative interview data contained the participants' experiences, opinions, feelings, and personal information. In phenomenological studies, "the participants must be individuals who have all experienced the phenomenon being explored and can articulate their lived experiences" (Creswell, 2007, p. 119). The interviews produced natural data from participants who had the ability to provide information on their lived experiences of the phenomenon that was studied. Based on the ArcGIS model (complete system for managing and designing solutions), the use of qualitative questions facilitates the interview process. Qualitative questions have been applied in past studies to derive reliable, experience-based information.

In a study performed by Amori (2010), the use of qualitative questions helped to illustrate the experiences of moral leadership within contemporary public schools. In another study, Pizarro (2010) used qualitative questions that helped to explore the lived experiences of the participants of the Latin origin and the implications of those experiences. Using the methodology, researchers have investigated life-transitioning experiences of senior military officers after retirement and their return to civilian society (Savion, 2009). The use of open-ended questions was similarly applied in order to gather data on the peer-teaching experiences of older adults in the study (Choi, 2007). Similarly, Kroch (2009) employed qualitative questioning to explore the life experiences of those living with the military-related trauma.

This chapter describes the ways in which the qualitative phenomenological technique was used and its importance as a framework for the study.

A phenomenological study is one in which an exploration is performed whereby multifaceted and meaningful data can be mined, and which can result in the development of clear conclusions (Anderson & Spenser, 2002).

Population and Sampling Procedures

The research project used the stakeholder approach and purposive sampling technique. Such an approach implies that the most effective study participants were Sudanese refugees, who were the major target of this study. Participants were drawn from a pool of Sudanese refugees (stakeholders) currently living in the United States. The individuals benefited from this study by contributing their life experiences, thus allowing the researchers to determine the magnitude of the problems they have suffered and the impacts these problems have had on their life status, perceptions, and attitudes.

No preconditions were required regarding the identification and selection of the study participants. The technique, however, required the study participants to have lived through experiences relevant to the Sudanese conflicts. In order to derive relevant and viable information, the study involved participants who were willing to contribute to this study.

Access and Permission Information

Before starting the interview, the confidentiality and anonymity guidelines were explained to the participants, any questions about the nature of the interview were answered, and the use of consent forms was explained. Participants were reminded that participation was voluntary and that the decision to withdraw carried no penalty. Participants were provided with the contact information of a local counselor or grief services agency in the event that they may find the interview process bringing up feelings of grief. If a participant became overwhelmed and was unable to manage during the interview, the interview was terminated and the participant was directly referred to a grief services agency; fortunately this never happen.

As a whole, Moustakas' (1994) phenomenological approach eliminates the dehumanization of participants that can occur in research studies by elevating the status of the participant to the same level as that of the researchers while also creating an interactive relationship. Because Moustakas' (1994) model facilitates a process where the participant is seen as a core-searcher and expert, the participants are on equal footing with the lead analyst. This particular approach and research philosophy elevates the core-searcher to a greater level of autonomy. Additionally, Moustakas' (1994) strategy incorporates interactive interviews, which gives the participant the final word in how they frame their lived experiences. The result of this type of strategy is the fostering of an environment of dignity and empowerment for each of the participants.

Data Collection

Ten of the contacted participants volunteered to be interviewed and the participants were given any additional information that they required. The participants were told of the purpose of the study and the participants were required to fill out and sign an informed consent form and informed that they had the ability to withdraw from the study at any time. A letter that included a guarantee of confidentiality and other additional information accompanied this process. Each participant was given an appointment for his or her interview, which took place over a one-hour period. Participants were informed that a follow-up interview would be required in order to revisit or clarify any unresolved issues. All interviews were approximately the same length, and the process was the same for each interview. Each participant was asked a series of open-ended questions about his or her background, experiences in Sudan, and subsequent experiences.

All interviews were digitally recorded. The digital recordings were then submitted to a professional transcriptionist for transcription. Confidentiality was maintained by having the transcriptionist sign a nondisclosure agreement, and no names were used in the interviews to ensure that the transcriptionist would not be able to identify the participants. Transcripts of the interviews were presented to the researcher in three forms: the original digital recording, a digital copy of the typed/word-processed interview, and a hard copy of the interview. Field notes were also recorded. The field notes were collected on a laptop computer using Microsoft Word. These notes were secured with a password, both in their raw and reported forms. The laptop was kept with the researcher at all times. Given the stated research methods, only verbalized cues or comments were included as raw data for this research; no gestures or demonstrations performed by the participant during the interview were incorporated into the data for coding or entered into the results.

Collection and interpretation of the data incorporated Moustakas' (1994) four key processes: (a) epoche, (b) transcendental-phenomenological reduction, (c) imaginative variation, and (d) synthesis. Moustakas' model, which incorporates reflective discussion and interactions between the researcher and participant, led to a foundation of the collected data that was analyzed.

Epoche

Moustakas' (1994) model of epoche is a process that helps the researcher put aside any pre-existing ideas about the subject matter and the participants in order to ensure that no judgments, theories, or ideologies are able to infiltrate the researcher's interpretations of the participants' experiences as they are explained by the participants. To this end, the epoche technique was initiated at the beginning of the study process and sustained throughout the interview process to ensure that there were few misunderstandings when interpreting the data disclosed during the interviews. The process was achieved by ensuring that the research takes a skeptical approach to information already known about the external world and the conflict in Sudan and, instead, focuses on only the personal information presented by the participants during the interviews.

Transcendental-Phenomenological Reduction

Transcendental-phenomenological reduction, the second of the four processes, helps the researcher to perceive clearly the lived experiences. This phenomenon allows the researcher to develop an accurate, context-based description of the participants' messages. In this way, the central idea is that phenomenology, as a methodology, needs to focus on the essence of the lived experience; however, this methodology also requires a scientific approach. The researcher must be able not only to transcribe, but also to translate the ideas put forward by the participants so that the underlying character and meaning of their lived experiences can be captured. Husserl (1931) referred to this process as a form of meditation, requiring rigorous, persistent effort and focus. Such focus can be achieved by the researcher diligently clearing his or her mind of all extraneous information so that only scientific inquiry, rather than assessments or analyses of the given information, governs the interviews.

Imaginative Variation

The third component of the methodology, Moustakas' (1994) imaginative variation, requires the researcher to reflect upon the character and meaning of the participants' lived experiences to ensure that a structural description of the fundamental data can be communicated. This framework helps the researcher to perceive the fact that there is no objective truth; instead, the experiences reported by the participants can be codified in a way that communicates the truth that each person knows based on his or her own unique life history. Achieving this goal requires the researcher to reflect consciously on what is being said in the interviews, both during and after the data collection process.

Synthesis

The concluding step in the data collection process is what Moustakas (1994) calls the synthesis of meanings and essences, which is the integration of the textual and structural descriptions into a unified statement of the essence of the lived experiences of each participant. This process needs to occur during both the data collection process and data analysis. Because the meanings and essences that could be acquired by this study could be considered infinite, especially after a comprehensive and reflective study of the phenomena presented by participants, the textual-structural syntheses that was presented for data analysis symbolized the essences of the experience as reported at that particular moment and place from the point of view of each participant.

Data Analysis

As noted by Creswell (2007), how the participants are chosen for a study may "help the researcher to generate or discover a theory or specific concepts within the theory" (p. 205). Researchers develop such a theory through formulating concepts logically and systematically, explaining the specific study-observations using the collected data/information. Moustakas (1994) explained that interviews can help researchers make connections between fundamental themes and that "the interviewer/interviewee dialogue can be based on questions, sequential or historical recollections, individual stories, important incidents, actions, or issues of moral and legal matter" (p. 44).

The transcripts must be examined through the phenomenological framework (Churchill, 2006). The data analysis model that is used in this study is both empirical and phenomenological (Churchill, 2006), as shown by the study performed by Robbins and Parlavecchio (2006). The data analysis process for this research is made up of seven distinct steps, including: "(a) reading the descriptions, (b) seeing descriptions, (c) delineating units of meaning (i.e. thorough scrutiny of the critical data), (d) organizing the meaning units, (e) seeing the meaning units psychologically, (f) situating structural descriptions, (g) identifying general themes, and (h) constructing a general situated structure" (Robbins & Parlavecchio, 2006, p. 333).

Reading the descriptions and then delineating and organizing the meaning units required several distinct steps. First, every type of experience was listed and grouped according to the words used by participants. Inclusion in this list was tested using two criteria: (a) if the expression contained a description of the moment of the experience that was sufficient for understanding it and (b) if it was possible to abstract and label this experience. Overlapping, repetitive, and vague expressions were eliminated or presented using the best descriptive terms possible, according to their essence.

Robbins and Parlavecchio (2006) have written that the process of "seeing psychologically" (p. 334) is equated with the way in which a researcher interprets and understands a participant's ideas. The researcher can use the process of seeing psychologically to explore the participant's system of relationships and how the participant perceives his or her importance and value. This process requires the further expansion of ideas proposed by the participant, rather than the actual words that are used. It was important for the researcher to examine critically each participant's emotions when answering questions to ensure that the fundamental data on either his or her psychological experiences in the Sudan and later life could be codified. These experiences were clustered into thematic groups. These themes were checked against the contributions of each participant using the following criteria: (a) if the themes were explicitly expressed in each participant's transcript; and (b) if the themes were compatible, even if they were not explicitly expressed. If the themes were not explicit or compatible in this manner, then it was concluded that they were not relevant to the participant's experience and were removed from the study analysis (Moustakas, 1994).

Once the themes and meaning units were identified, structural descriptions and a general codified structure were created. Contextual descriptions of each interview were developed, with verbatim examples from the transcribed interviews included where necessary. From such examples, a composite structural description was developed, drawing on the meaning and essence of each experience, allowing the construction of a representation of the group as a whole. Data collection and analysis occurred co-currently for inter-dependence purposes. This occurred through determining what researchers have already discovered, what was still under investigation by researchers, and the existing gaps in the research world by applying an iterative research process.

The final stage of the examination consisted of pulling all of this information together for synthesis. As noted above, the process of synthesizing meanings and essences, which is the integration of textual and structural descriptions into a unified statement of the essence of the lived experiences of participants, needed to be repeated at this point in the study, that is, after the codification of the data and reflection on its meaning. This data and the subsequent development of the information gained by this effort was used to move towards a theoretical understanding, rather than letting a theory guide the research process. Once the themes were solidified, it was possible to draw conclusions about the meaning of the data. These conclusions were compared to the original research question and recommendations were made.

Validity

Validity can be ascertained in a phenomenological research study by using data-capturing methods that are intrinsically linked to the purpose of the study (Salkind, 2003). For this study, the validity of the interview questions can be ascertained by using 7-10 participants who meet the criteria for involvement (Creswell, 2009). Changes to the questions used in the interviews may occur as the research progresses in order to guarantee that the contributions of the participants accurately represent the needs of the research study, as each individual may have a different way of responding to each question. Different forms of responses do not mean that external validity will not be a problem, as the number of participants in the chosen sample will be limited.

At the same time, researchers have made a point of emphasizing the "truth value" of qualitative interviews and the value of external validity (Schurink, Schurink, & Poggenpoel, 1998). Nevertheless, for the sake of gaining the advantages associated with phenomenological research, the meaning of the data collected should not be extrapolated to a broader population than is warranted, even if the data is robust (Creswell, 2009). In phenomenological epistemology, therefore, a balance needs to be found between the meanings, values, and themes that can be derived from self-reports (Robbins & Parlavecchio, 2006). Nevertheless, this approach can form the foundation of ideas that can be used in further research in the study area. Building on this framework for validity and analysis, it is evident that the present research methodology was the best fit for this study.

Reliability

Most of the assurance required for data reliability was acquired using the validity and verification processes outlined above. However, Golafshani (2003) highlighted the importance of assuring the consistency of results through the accurate representation of reproducible efforts if the results of the research are to be considered to be based upon reliable data. Therefore, consistent with Golafshani's (2003) suggestions, the following processes were integrated into this research effort. The units of data measurement remained the same throughout the course of the research effort, including the interpretation of subjective terms such as "frequently," "occasionally," "often," "rarely," and so forth. Consistency in the units of data measurement is particularly important when using a phenomenological approach. Consistently asking the same questions, particularly when utilizing open-ended interviews, was required to ensure consistent responses. Again, given the nature of the current research effort and the processes that were required for coding the responses given during the interview process, this was a critical process for assuring reliable data.

CHAPTER FOUR

DATA ANALYSIS

This chapter contains the results of the phenomenological qualitative research study involving 10 Sudanese individuals living in South Dakota in the United States. The 10 participants were all part of Sudan's lost generation. The purpose of this study was to explore the lived experiences of the lost boys and girls and present their experiences through phenomenological research, thus allowing their stories to provide an understanding into the nature and effect of the experience of being a child soldier. Data for this study was collected using qualitative interviews to help in understanding the challenges and barriers of Sudanese lost generation members in South Dakota.

Drawing from the qualitative interviews, this chapter is focused on highlighting challenges and experiences of the lost Sudanese generation, such as navigating unfamiliar social, cultural, educational, and legal systems as reflected in the interviews. The collected data were focused on psychological the lived experiences and trauma among the lost Sudanese generation members as narrated by the participants. Thus, the results discussed in this chapter do not include any prior knowledge from other literature or previous studies on the same subject. The analysis relied on the experiences of the participants as narrated during the interviews. The first section of this chapter provides a description of each participant. The second section outlines the process of organizing the qualitative data for analysis and the resultant codes and themes. The themes are then discussed in detail.

Participants

The study involved three female participants and seven male participants living in South Dakota. Although previous qualitative phenomenological studies have used varying sampling sizes, this study only engaged 10 participants. The study participants were Sudanese refugees who currently live in South Dakota but originate from the peasant backgrounds of Southern Sudan. The demographic characteristics of each participant are given below.

Participant 1 is a 32-year-old female from the Juba tribe in Sudan. She currently works as an office assistant in one of the accounting firms in South Dakota. She speaks fluently in her mother tongue, but she has also learned to communicate in English while living in the U.S. The participant is one of the child soldiers that managed to survive the war and move to the Kakuma camp in Kenya. She was rescued by U.N. peacekeepers that later assisted her to travel to America.

She has managed to complete her secondary education and study office administration while living in America. She lives with her Sudanese foster parents, who moved to America before the war started. The participant does not belong to any specific religion, but she is drawn to Christian faith. This is the dominant religion in South Dakota.

Participant 2 is a 27-year-old male who is married to another Sudanese who has been living in the U.S. A. Both the participant and the wife are from the Juba tribe. They came to America with the help of U.N. peacekeepers from one of the refugee camps in Sudan. The participant is pursuing his college education and works part time jobs to sustain his family. He is a Christian and has been separated from his family since he joined the army. He is comfortable living in the U.S. and is unwilling to go back to his country.

Participant 3 is a 30-year-old male, a Dinka by tribe from Sudan. He is married with children and works as an accountant. He lost his family in the war and has no plans of going back to Sudan. Despite the many years that have passed since he escaped from the war, he still suffers from the trauma of having participated in it. He moved to the U.S. with the help of the United Nations High Commissioner for Refugees (UNHCR) and was placed in foster care until he completed his college education. He is still undergoing therapy and counseling for posttraumatic stress disorder and "appreciates their impact on his emotional health".

Participant 4 is a 25-year-old male from the Aweil tribe who left Sudan for Kakuma as an injured soldier. He lived in the camp for a while before UNHCR recruited him as one of their workers and facilitated his travel to the U.S. Since he was used to a different educational system, it was very hard for him to complete his education in the U.S. The war began before he could finish his primary education, and he was forced to join the army as a child soldier. After finishing college, he was unable to secure employment. He could only find temporary jobs but was unemployed at the time of the interview. He has no information of his family, but he intends to go back to Sudan and look for them.

Participant 5 is a 28-year-old male from the Wau tribe in Sudan who was working at a cement company at the time of the interview. He is comfortable being away from home because of the peace and a better standard of living. He is single and does not belong to any religion. He is one of the soldiers that sustained serious injuries in the war. The participant managed to complete his secondary education in the U.S.

Participant 6 is a 24-year-old male from the Aweil tribe. Since he moved to the U.S., he has only managed to complete his secondary education and thus has no professional skills. Lack of education has limited his ability to access formal employment. He was a violent teenager who could not get along with his foster parents, and he is now living alone in South Dakota. Their disagreements limited his chances of accessing higher education.

Participant 7 is a 26-year-old woman living with her husband in South Dakota. She has no formal education, and she is still learning English as a second language. She is from the Dinka tribe in Sudan. She cannot find work due to lack of education. She does not belong to any particular religion and has no knowledge of the location of her family. She is among the Sudanese who had a rough time in the U.S. due to a lack of a basic education and a stable source of income. Her foster parents separated, and she had to live on the streets.

Participant 8 is a 29-year-old male who was working temporary job at the time of the interview. The participant is one of Sudanese who managed to reunite with their families after the war. His family travelled to the U.S. soon after he travelled as a UNHCR worker. He has not managed to complete his college education due to a lack of finances, and he has to support his family as well. He is a Muslim, and he partly blames his religious background for both the suffering he experienced in Sudan and his unemployment in the U.S. He is from the Juba tribe in Sudan.

Participant 9 is a 31-year-old male who was captured from a wealthy Dinka family to become a child soldier. He managed to reunite with his family, who came to the U.S. after the war but went back to Sudan when peace returned. He is married, a Christian, and struggling to care for his family due to unemployment. At the time of the interview, he was planning to pursue higher education in order to offer a better life to his family.

Participant 10 is a 35-year-old female who was captured by the militia and forced to take care of the soldiers at the camp. She was working in a security firm at the time of the interview. Her foster parents managed to educate her, and this helped her to find a well paying job in the U.S. She was a Muslim before the war broke, but she converted to Christianity while in the U.S. She is from the Dinka tribe in Sudan.

Overview

Although previous qualitative phenomenological studies have used varying sampling sizes, this study only engaged 10 participants. The study participants were Sudanese refugees who currently live in South Dakota but originate from the peasant backgrounds of Southern Sudan. Most of the participants were born around 1983. This population includes persons from communities and settlements surrounding Aweil, Juba, and Wau and predominantly identify with the Dinka tribe. The 10 study participants were between 20-37 years of age. Interviews were the primary data collection tool used in this study. The researchers selected a private area where the interviews took place, such as library or business meeting rooms normally used for secluded conversations (Van Manen, 2007). The demographic data concerning the participants is resumed in the below table:

Table 2
Demographic Data

Participants	Age	Gender	Educational level	Faith	Tribe	Marital Status
Participant 1	32	Female	College	Christian	Juba	Single
Participant 2	27	Male	College	Christian	Juba	Married
Participant 3	30	Male	College	None	Dinka	Married
Participant 4	25	Male	College	None	Aweil	Single
Participant 5	28	Male	Secondary education	None	Wau	Single
Participant 6	24	Male	Secondary Education	None	Aweil	Single
Participant 7	26	Female	None	None	Dinka	Married
Participant 8	29	Male	College	Muslim	Juba	Single
Participant 9	31	Male	College, planning to pursue higher education	Christian	Dinka	Married
Participant 10	35	Female	College	Christian (former Muslim)	Dinka	Single

Data Analysis

The data used in this phenomenological study consisted of the words, phrases, and sentences spoken by each participant in individual face-to-face interviews. Each study participant was asked the same set of 18 questions (see Appendix). Each interview was audio tape-recorded, and transcriptions were typed by a transcriptionist with the verbatim responses for each individual. Giorgi (2006) noted that there were five steps in the analysis of the phenomenological scientific method. These steps include: "(a) collection of verbal data, (b) reading of the data, (c) breaking of the data into some kind of parts, (d) organization and expression of the data from a disciplinary perspective, and (e) synthesis or summary of the data for the purposes of communication to the scholarly community" (p. 245).

Giorgi (2006) notes the first step of collecting the data is through description, interview, or both. Individuals are asked open-ended questions and encouraged to share their experiences or views. The second step as noted by Giorgi is reading the data. Reading the data provides the analyst with a view of the data as a whole, and no attempt is made to identify what is important in the data. The third step for breaking down the data will typically take the perspective of the origination of the study. Units with meaning are then identified in the text of the transcripts and are in line with the basis of the study, either psychological or sociological. The object is to find meaning in the data. The fourth step organizes the data into a disciplinary perspective. The participant's language is transformed to the "relevant scientific discipline" (Giorgi, 2006, p. 247). Giorgio's fifth step, synthesis, involves describing the essential structure of the participants' experiences from the perspective of the scientific discipline.

A systematic inductive approach to the analysis incorporating Giorgi's (2006) precepts was used in the analysis of the data collected for this study. Braun and Clarke (2006) noted that thematic analysis "captures something important about the data in relation to the research question, and represents some level of patterned response or meaning within the data set" (p. 10). When contemplating the data, it is important to contemplate what constitutes a theme and how large that theme is both within each item and across all data. Just because there are a number of instances of a theme, it does not mean that it is more important than one with fewer instances. The important thing is whether the theme captures the essence of the data in reference to the research questions. Themes or patterns can be identified inductively or deductively (Braun & Clarke, 2006).

In using an inductive approach, themes are related to the data (Patton, 2002). As in this study, the data was collected specifically for this particular study, and there was no attempt to fit the data into preconceived themes or categories/codes. Braun and Clarke (2006) noted that inductive thematic analysis can occur at the semantic or explicit levels. This researcher chose to use the semantic approach for this study and not to move beyond what was said in the interviews. The analysis begins with reading and noticing or looking for ideas, constructs, and meaning in the data and making notes as the reading commences. This process involves constant comparison between the data and the themes or coded bits of data. It is also possible that two themes might essentially be the same and might need to be combined into one theme. Themes are named and defined, while mapping the data may provide a visual of how the themes relate to each other and may assist in identifying what is interesting in the themes.

The raw data that were included in the analysis consisted of verbalized responses from the participants. It did not include any gestures and demonstrations from participants as they answered the interview questions. The data analysis in this section did not include any pre-existing theories about the war in Sudan. The researcher relied solely on the responses from participants.

Giorgi (2006, p. 245) discussed the phenomenological research method in detail and outlined five major steps that researchers should follow when using this method. These steps include:

1. Collecting verbal data
2. Reading the data
3. Breaking the data into parts
4. Organization and expression of the data from a disciplinary perspective
5. Synthesis of the data

These steps were followed in collecting and analyzing qualitative data in this study. Each step is discussed in detail below.

Collecting Verbal Data

In this study, verbal data were collected through face-to-face interviews with the participants. Participants were able to use English clearly enough for efficient communication. The questions asked were open-ended, which allowed the participants to give as much information as they could for each question. The researcher gave the participants enough time to answer each question to obtain a detailed account of their experiences as child soldiers. Participants gave their descriptions of their experiences during the war, and the interview questions allowed the researcher to seek clarification and further elaboration of each description. Each interview was recorded using a digital video camera. The questions and responses were then transcribed for analysis.

Reading the Data

After obtaining the transcribed data, the researcher read all the responses from all the participants. This reading was necessary to obtain a general idea of the participants' responses. The researcher did not attempt to derive any themes at this stage.

Breaking the Data into Parts

The second reading of the transcribed data was coupled with an in-depth analysis of each response to identify any meaningful units. The meaningful units in this case represented any expression of what the participants went through before, during, and after the war. The researcher highlighted all irrelevant responses and grouped them with the corresponding participants for future responses. Irrelevant responses were reconsidered to determine whether there was any meaningful information or further elaboration. The researcher developed and placed different codes on the meaning units on the relevant responses. Each time a meaning unit was identified, it was coded with an existing or new code depending on its description. The codes assigned to the meaningful units or participants' experiences were inductive. The codes that were developed in the analysis and their abbreviations are summarized in the table below. Some of the corresponding responses from participants are included as well.

Table 3
Codes for Participant Responses

Code/Category	Abbreviation	Participant Responses
Discontinuation from school	DS	I stopped going to school. We even stopped going to school. No more schooling. We could not go to school.
Separation from family members	SF	During the war, my father was killed, my mother fled with 2 of my sisters and we did not manage to reconnect after the war. My sister died during the war it remains one of my worst nightmares. My parents were separated and the rest of my siblings lived on their own.
Coercion to become a child soldier	CS	They take us with my friends when us we are grazing my father's cattle and playing. Then they beat us and force us to enter in their track. They take me to be a soldier. We were captured from home as I already said. But before were trained they think some will run away or retort, so they beat us up, pierced us with weapons and shot some and we had to accept that there is no running away.

(continued)

Table 3 (continued)

Code/Category	Abbreviation	Participant Responses
Physical violence directly to child soldiers	PV	Beat us up, pierced us with weapons and shot some. They beat us and put us in their tracks. First, we were tortured to accept their way. We were constantly beaten ruthlessly.
Rape	RP	And he raped me badly. I was raped countless times. They raped me, seven of them.
Emotional distress and trauma	ED	Sometimes I felt hopeless. I was so bitter and frightened. I felt like an animal.

| Physical displacement | PD | We are displaced from our home at Sudan, me and my other siblings then we are took to Ethiopia.
I left Sudan.
We were always on the run; never had a permanent home. |
| Mixed emotions after leaving Sudan | | It was a mixture of feelings.
It is peaceful here and better than Sudan. . . It is not the same. . . at least we are safe Happy, missing their country, safety, employment. |

(continued)

Table 3 (continued)

Code/Category	Abbreviation	Participant Responses
Relationship issues	RL	I have very few friends. I never trusted anyone. It is hard for me to make new friends and keep them. I don't want to get married.
Additional family responsibilities	FR	Me and my brothers we would sleep outside to make sure we that provide security for my mother and sister.
Physical suffering	PS	We did not have food. We slept out in the cold most of times. We used to walk for long distances I was shot in the arm and I had to bear all the pain.
Attitude toward religions	REL	Although am not Christian, I do have very bad feelings against the Islamic people. I was Muslim. It contributed greatly to my suffering and displacement in Sudan. It partially contributed to my suffering. . . Christians discriminated the Muslims.
Reasons for the war		There were tensions about religion differences and economic differences. People started to preach unfairness in distribution of income, differences between religion and all that. I not very sure that religion was the reason but it could have contributed.

(continued)

Table 3 (continued)

Code/Category	Abbreviation	Participant Responses
Witnessing violence	WV	These soldiers raped women and young girls as we watched.
		Two others shot at my parents, my three sisters and my youngest brother while I watched.
		Five of the other children soldiers were forced to kill their own parents and small sisters.
Missing parental love and family environment	FC	I miss my family very much.
		I lost my family.
Difficulties in adjusting to a new live in the U.S.	DF	Underemployment and unemployment are the major challenges. However, those with education are sometimes humiliated working at very low profile jobs.
		If there was no war, I would prefer to live in Sudan especially with my family.

The abbreviations were used to mark the meaningful units. For instance, every time the researcher came across a description that indicated that the participant stopped going to school, the researcher would mark that sentence with the abbreviation DS. Coding the responses from the participants was a challenge because some of the meaning units could fit into more than one code. After coding all the relevant responses and eliminating all irrelevant descriptions, the researcher grouped all responses according to their codes. For instance, all the responses marked with DS were grouped together. The researcher did not only rely on the participants' descriptions to develop the codes.

Organization and Expression of the Data from a Disciplinary Perspective

Participants gave concrete descriptions of their experiences as child soldiers. These descriptions helped the researcher to identify any emerging themes. In addition to these descriptions, the researcher adopted a psychological perspective to narrow down the identified meaning units. A sociological perspective was also necessary to transform some of the meaning units, especially on relationships. Applying a disciplinary perspective on the meaning units was necessary to identify any patterns and themes that participants insinuated with their descriptions. For instance, none of the participants stated clearly that they were suffering from posttraumatic stress disorder. In fact, most of them indicated that they received treatment and therapy and they were now living a normal life. However, using a psychological perspective to analyze the meaning units helped the researcher to discover that some participants were still suffering from posttraumatic stress disorder. Such a theme would have been left out if the researcher solely relied on the participants' descriptions.

Synthesis of the Data

The codes developed in the previous steps were further regrouped and compressed to identify the emerging themes. However, the identification of themes was not limited to grouping different codes together. The researcher used a theoretical perspective to identify themes from an overall analysis of all the responses from participants. The major themes that were developed from the raw data include:

1. Disruption of life
2. Physical suffering
3. Trauma and emotional distress

Each of these themes is discussed in detail below.

Disruption of Life.

The war disrupted the lives of the child soldiers in many ways. The aspects of their disrupted lives that the participants described include education, family units, and physical location. Each of these aspects is discussed below.

One of the major disruptions in the lives of the lost boys and girls was the discontinuation of formal education. Most of the lost generation of Sudanese boys and girls stopped formal schooling, and others did not even begin formal education in South Dakota. Education became a point of stress and depression for those Sudanese refugees who had begun their education and had to stop following the war outbreak while they stayed in refugee camps and other reserved refugee areas in which education was not the first priority, but rather needs such as food and clothing took precedence. One of the participants indicated that he and his friends were forcefully captured from school to join the army. This is how he described the experience: "I was forced after kidnapping from school as a young boy of 12 years and I was so badly injured by the soldiers and almost died." Another participant indicated, "we lived in fear because we did not know what would happen. We even stopped going to school." Because the participants were child soldiers, their primary level of education was disrupted and some only managed to complete their education after leaving Sudan. One participant described her experience as follows:

> I was still young and used to go to primary school. . . . One day, we were walking home from school with my friends from school . . . we saw a truck come from the bush and we were forced to get into it by the soldiers who were in it . . . we were dropped somewhere at a camp that had so many soldiers, I knew things were bad.

When the war broke, family units were disintegrated. Every participant in this study indicated that he or she was separated from family members. Some of them lost their family members and some had never traced their family since the war broke. One participant stated, "I do not have a family. I do not know because it is difficult to find my father, mother, and other five sisters and brothers. You even do not know if they are alive." Another participant indicated:

> There was a family with Dad and other five children, but not anymore. Prior to war, we had a peaceful and good family. We had what we needed. Not very rich, but what you would call a middle class family. There was a lot of love and

cooperation from our parents because they took us to school daily, had some days
out together; you know the things families do together. Three children of us were
schooling and two were still very young. It is painful we cannot see each other
now, and may be, not anymore. All the rest are back in Sudan I think, and I fear
some are no more, following the war [*sic*].

One of the most painful experiences for the participants was watching their family members die.
Some were even forced to kill their family members. One participant narrated his experience as
follows:

One day in the evening, a few of the militia men took me and accompanied me to
my home. They ordered my parents and siblings to all line up outside our house.
One of the soldiers held me and two others shot at my parents, my three sisters,
and my youngest brother while I watched.

One participant watched her sister being burned alive, and stated "my sister, me watch her burnt
alive," while another witnessed the death of her parents, and stated, "Unfortunately, I went to
witness the death of my parents."

By forcing these children to watch their family members dying, the older soldiers were
making sure that the child soldiers would not escape from the camp or retreat from the war.
The experiences created fear in the child soldiers, and they had to stay in the army to stay alive.
Escaping from the army camp was too risky for the child soldiers, and some had no families or
homes to which to return. One participant stated, "You think you will be the next one on the line,
but you must do everything to live." One of the participants had been lucky enough to reunite
with some family members. Although his father died in the war, the participant was able to trace
his mother and sister.

Some of the participants indicated that they were brought up and educated by their foster
parents in the U.S. One stated, "Right now, I consider my foster parents to be my family
[*sic*]." Three of the participants (all men) indicated that they were married, and this brought
back memories of the family life that was disrupted by the war. The married participants were
protective of their families and did not want them to have a similar experience. One of the married
participants stated:

I am married with two children. I married a woman from Sudan. As I mentioned,
the way people treat each other here is very different. And you know, my wife
can understand me better because she knows the pain we went through to come
here. I don't want my children to experience what I went through. That gives me
a reason to want to stay here instead of go[*sic*] home.

All the participants indicated that they were displaced from their homes in Sudan. One of the
participants was displaced from his home to a refugee camp in Sudan. Another participant
indicated that he ran away from Sudan to Ethiopia and then back to a refugee camp in Sudan.
The other eight participants indicated that they were either assisted by peacekeepers or walked
for long distances to the Kakuma camp in Kenya. The study involved the Sudanese lost boys and
girls living in South Dakota. This means that they are still physically displaced from their homes

in Sudan. The first displacement of the child soldiers was from their homes to army camps. Some of the soldiers managed to escape, while some were rescued by U.N. peacekeepers. The soldiers ended up in refugee camps and finally in the U.S., which is their current residence.

Two of the participants indicated that they were displaced many times before they could move out of Sudan to Kenya. One of them explained, "Since the day I joined the militia group, we were always on the run; never had a permanent home apart from the one I knew before my family was wiped out. Later I moved from Sudan to Kenya." The other participant described the experience, "Since the time we were captured, we never had a permanent home. We moved from forest to forest with these soldiers."

Physical Suffering.

Each of the participants experienced physical pain or discomfort during the war. The three women interviewed indicated that they were raped on several occasions during the war. One of the women who participated in the study indicated that her fellow soldiers in the camp raped her severely. She described her experience saying that "the soldier told that girl to step away from where I was, and he raped me badly. After that another soldier came and raped me again." This experience had long-term effects on the participant, especially with establishing relationships with men. She was unwilling to marry a man and preferred to live with a woman to avoid another rape. She stated:

> I don't want to get married, I will not be raped again no. But you know, I am afraid of living on my own. I do not know maybe I can find a friend (woman) who I can live with [*sic*]. Men are not very good.

The other female participant experienced more than rape in one incident that she described in the following words: "they rape me, they beat me, have my left arm ache due to them beating me [*sic*]." The third female participant was raped as she escaped to a refugee camp. In her words, "I was raped countless times by the male colleagues we were with during our travel from Sudan to Kakuma Refugee camp."

One common form of suffering among the participants was the violence of the senior soldiers in camp. The child soldiers were beaten as a way of threatening them to remain within the camp. Only three of the participants joined the army willingly, thinking that it was the right thing to do to protect their country. The other seven participants indicated that they were coerced into joining the army. They were captured as young boys and girls with no fighting skills. Their training was coupled with beatings and harassments from the senior soldiers. The child soldiers had to learn how to survive the harassment from other soldiers. The women were forced to cook for the soldiers in the camp. One soldier recounted his experience in the camp as follows:

> After the National Islamic Front soldiers captured me... I still remember the uncountable times I was beaten and you can see the scars all over my body. This was done in an exclusion with any kind of tools they had [*sic*]. That is before we accepted to train as soldiers. They pierce you and threaten you with weapons and beat you up before and even during training.

Another participant who experienced ruthless beatings from senior soldiers described his experience as follows:

> They cut us, pierce us with all manner of weapons and drag us around, naked. Some guys were shot mercilessly as you watch. So, you can't imagine the torture in the hands of National Islamic Front and the need to survive, whether you are in training or not, whether you are already bleeding or fresh, whether you are young or old. There were the wounds and the pain, and worst is fear of losing your life at any time. You hear the shots but you don't know if you are the target [*sic*].

These experiences pushed some of the soldiers to escape from the camp while some were left to die when they became too weak to fight. Some sustained serious injuries and were only lucky to live because the U.N. peacekeepers found them in time.

Another form of physical suffering that the soldiers experienced was hunger. The soldiers did not have enough food in either the army camp or the refugee camps. They also faced extreme weather conditions, which affected their health. Being in the army involved walking for long distances through forests as the soldiers ran from or pursued their enemies. One participant recounted such experiences and stated:

> Soldiers were expected to be strong with or without food. Most of the times we did not have food. We slept out in the cold most of times guarding the senior soldiers. The little food that was brought in the camp it was first given to the NMF soldiers. When we were going to fight, the lorry that was there only carried the NMF soldiers, us we used to walk for long distances. I remember one day we were walking in the forest, I stepped on a snake. By good luck, it did not bite me so deep and I think it was not poisonous so I survived. Also, we were constantly beaten ruthlessly sometimes without a reason. I think they wanted us to become rough like them.

Trauma and Emotional Distress.

The horrible experiences of the child soldiers during the war brought about emotional distress and trauma. Some of the participants' descriptions of their feelings about their experiences indicated that the events were traumatizing. For instance, the soldiers witnessed people die, including their family members and friends. Some were forced to watch their family members die while some were forced to kill their own people as a way of showing their loyalty to the army. Every participant witnessed some form of physical violence and experienced the same. This had an effect on their emotional states. One of the soldiers who was forced to kill his friends recounted, "I remember shooting two of my friends we used to school with [*sic*] . . . I felt like an animal."

Due to the distress experienced by the soldiers some developed anger while some contemplated suicide. One such participant recounted, "I had a lot of pain and anger. I saw them as enemies. Sometimes I felt like suicide would be better to relieve the pain and memories of bad things I did [*sic*]." Another described his feelings during the war in the following words: "I felt undermined, rejected and angry. . . . I was so bitter and frightened." There was also a feeling of helplessness, as one participant described, "I felt very desperate." Such desperation was common among child soldiers because most of them were forced to join the army and had no way out. The senior soldiers overpowered them, and retreating meant death. Even the soldiers who joined the army voluntarily later realized that the soldiers had lied to them about the war. One of the volunteers recounted his feelings about the militia killing his parents as he watched and said, "I would have killed these militia men."

Some of the soldiers felt guilty for their actions, especially those who were forced to kill their family members or friends. One soldier was forced to kill women and girls who had been raped by the senior soldiers. He described his feelings toward that experience in the following words:

> These soldiers raped women and young girls as we watched. After they finished, they forced us to kill them. I, I, I, I remember I was forced to shoot a lady after they had gang-raped her at gunpoint and she was expecting. I knew her . . . it seemed to me this was a very long nightmare. To bring this nightmare to an end, I thought it was good that I get used to it but anytime I killed, I felt more guilty [*sic*].

One other participant described his psychical trauma as a result of having been forced to kill people in the following way: "I know I had no choice, but I am haunted by the faces of those I killed. Sometimes, I didn't even get to see their faces, but they haunt me anyway. I wish I could remove those images from my head." Another participant indicated that he was afraid to go back to Sudan and face the families of the people he killed. He stated, "I will always feel guilty when I see the family members of the people I killed. Let me stay here."

Furthermore, participants described their experiences as abused youth differently and used different techniques to cope with it. One of them experienced great anger and explicitly said that she would have killed those who hurt her: "I think I would have killed my rapists if I could. Even now, when I think about it, I feel uncontrollable rage. I hate it that I could not cause those horrible men the same pain they caused to me." Another participant however, coped by detaching from the situation. She described her experience in the following way: "I tried to imagine that I was in a happy place, like home, while I was being raped. I sometimes felt like leaving my own body and watching everything with no feeling." Her out-of-body experience was a result of her incapacity to defend herself from the abusers and acted as a defense mechanism (Blume, 1990).

The participants also proved resilient when talking about their families being killed in front of them. Some could not talk about it at all, and others started crying and could not continue. To the interviewer's question regarding the death of his family, one participant refused to answer, saying "I don't think I can, I am sorry. . . it hurts a lot! Can we take a break?" Another participant concluded: "And I feel pain about my family. I hope they are alive [*sic*]."

In their quest for a better life, education is extremely important and has a role in maintaining and improving their mental health. The participants who were younger when they arrived and therefore could pursue an education, were not only more optimistic about their futures but also healthier and more communicative. Finally, one participant proved to be particularly communicative, and this too helped him to recover faster and to have positive results. He explained that he made new friends and talked a lot with other lost boys and girls, sharing their experiences. Communication and being able to communicate easily facilitates healing, while remaining isolated and keeping everything for oneself is extremely harmful.

However, the degree to which interviewees were able to rise above the experiences and rebuild a solid sense of self varied widely. Some of the participants mentioned nightmares, guilt, depression, and other signs of psychological trauma as part of their experiences. One participant described the resultant feelings by stating that "the experiences I went through made me vulnerable to anger, fear, bitterness, and insecurity."

Participants indicated that therapy was useful as a guide for thinking about who they had been before suffering the psychological trauma, as well as for thinking about their strength and resilience throughout the traumatic experiences. Therapy was a tool through which they were able to perceive the kind of people they could become in the future. One such participant stated:

> When I came, the first thing that happened was that we were taken through counseling and talking therapy together with others. It has helped me a lot. There was a time I used to think I don't want to live. Now I have changed, and don't want to die quickly.

The participants in the study recognized the efforts of various organizations, individuals, and government programs to help the lost girls and boys of Sudan rebuild their shattered senses of self-worth, which had resulted from traumatic experiences during and after the war. Counseling was identified as the most common form of support given to the participants. Most of the participants indicated that counseling had been useful for enabling them to address anger, stress, and other emotional imbalances, which had made them better people in the community. One of the key issues identified during data collection was that the participants particularly described themselves in terms of the suffering and the trauma they had experienced during the war.

The experiences of the child soldiers affect their way of relating with other people. One participant indicated that he still had bad feelings about his involvement in the war and preferred to be alone. In his words:

> I feel I cannot relate freely with others if I was taken back because of the fear in Sudan. You do not know who your enemy is. It is difficult here in South Dakota with new neighborhood although it would take time to form new friends. Many times, I still want to be alone and reflect about what happened because it still disturbs in mind [*sic*].

Some of the participants indicated that they had problems trusting other people. In fact, one of the women that participated in the study indicated that she was unwilling to get married due to the incidences of sexual harassment and rape that she experienced during the war. Therapy has helped most of the participants to open up to the people of South Dakota. Thus, the participants have managed to make new friends and adapt to the life in the U.S.

Analysis summary

The data is summarized in the below table.

Table 4
Data Summary

Disruption of life	Physical suffering	Trauma	PTSD and treatment
Disruption from family units	Rape	Anger	All participants received counseling for PTSD
Disruption from education	Beatings	Suicidal thoughts	Some participants received medication
Disruption from home	Torture	Guiltiness	All agreed as to the benefits of treatment
	Hunger	Painful memories	All doubted that they will ever be completely cured.
	Health issues	Fear	Ease of communication improves mental health
	Long walks	Lack of trust	Education or a clear purpose in life (like expecting a child) improves mental health.
		Out—of body experiences as a result of abuse	Lack of counseling and medication, when needed, had disastrous effects among the lost boys.
		Nightmares	
		Alcohol abuse	
		|Depression	

CHAPTER FIVE

DISCUSSION

The purpose of this study was to explore the lived experiences of the lost boys and girls of Sudan and present their experiences and the effect of those experiences on the lives of the participants at the time and later in their lives. A qualitative methodology with a phenomenological lens was used to design, conduct, analyze, and report the findings of the study. Ten individuals currently residing in Sioux Falls, South Dakota and who were immigrants from Sudan participated in the study. Each participant was interviewed individually and was asked the same 18 questions. Interview questions addressed (a) participants' lives before the war in Sudan, (b) participants' experiences during the war, and (c) participants' lived experiences after separation from warlike activities. The participants included three females and seven males ranging in age from 24 to 35 years (M = 28.7 years). Each participant had joined an army either voluntarily or involuntarily in the Sudanese conflict. Each participant also had escaped from or managed to leave the army and, through various routes, immigrate to the United States. In Chapter Five, the analysis of findings from data collected for the study are reviewed and related to the literature presented in earlier chapters. Recommendations for future research are presented and implications for practice with immigrants are discussed.

Findings and Discussion

Qualitative techniques have been used in the past to explore the experiences of immigrants (Pizarro, 2010), military personnel (Savion, 2009), leaders (Amori, 2010), peer teachers (Choi, 2007), and individuals with military related trauma (Kroch, 2009). A qualitative methodology was appropriate for exploring the experiences of this group of Sudanese immigrants to the United States. One research question was the guide for the data collection and analysis as follows: disruption and deprivation are common in conflict situations (Wesensten & Belenky, 2005). Wesensten and Blenkey (2005) also noted that conflict situations could have influence on cognitive performance. In addition to being deprived of their educational opportunities, cognitive performance interruptions had affected the growth and development of the study participants. While most of the participants had pursued or continued their education, it might be possible that those continuing their education would have changed their schemas (Beck, 1979).

Although loss of educational opportunities and the opportunity to learn for success in life were detrimental, the separation from families might have affected more profoundly the study participants. Beck (1979) believed that core beliefs are developed and reinforced in childhood to create schemas, of which families contribute to their development. If children are deprived of their families in the process of development, their positive or negative self-image may be affected. The current findings indicate that the participants did not always have a positive self-image, supporting Beck's (2005) ideas. Being forcefully removed from families and forced to do tasks the participants might never have done if this had not happened left deep impressions on them. The childhood wartime experiences of these now-adult participants, including being forcibly removed from their families, had an effect on them, their development, and their lives. Some participants wanted to return to Sudan to look for missing family members, but other participants did not want to return at all. That these participants might not have an opportunity to progress through the typical developmental stages had effects on them, as did their experiences as child soldiers in a war-torn country. All of these serve to support the findings of Beck and Giorgi as well.

Research Question

The researcher performed this study based on the following research question: What are the lived experiences of the lost boys and girls of Sudan who currently live in the United States?

A phenomenological approach was used in the collection of the data and analysis. The data was reviewed repeatedly, and notes were made before beginning the coding of the data. The data was coded in accordance with the philosophies and steps, as outlined by Giorgi (2006). The analysis showed three themes emerging from the data: (a) disruption of life, (b) physical suffering, (c) trauma and emotional distress. Each theme will be discussed in succession and related to the previously cited literature.

Disruption of Life

Most children follow a typical developmental sequence as they mature (Beck, 1979). The participants in the current study experienced a disruption in this developmental sequence regarding education, family life, physical and emotional development, and physical location. Each participant reported effects from separation from family and loss of educational opportunities. One participant commented on the new life in the U.S.:

> If there was no war, I would prefer to live in Sudan especially with my family here but now I don't have a family, if I go back I will be reminded of my past experiences and I am trying to forget. In addition, in Sudan it is easy to get a good job, it is not like here, I think it is because we are refugees, I don't know.

Children and families expect to have the opportunity to be together and to have an opportunity for formal education and socialization into society; however, because of the war in Sudan, these opportunities disappeared for the study participants. As children, the study participants were cut off from educational opportunities. As one participant describes:

> I didn't manage to finish school and no specific training, no good grammar but I hope to get a casual job that I can help myself and family if it will be there in future.

Disruption and deprivation are common in conflict situations (Wesensten & Belenky, 2005). For example, the participants in this study indicated that they could not access basic needs like food and shelter. One participant stated:

> Because of the difficult work we were doing at those camps, most of the times we did not have food, and repeated sexual harassment, one I grew so weak, collapsed and I think they damped me.

Wesensten and Blenkey (2005) also noted that conflict situations could influence cognitive performance. In addition to being deprived of their educational opportunities, cognitive performance interruptions had affected the growth and development of the study participants. For instance, all the participants were separated from their families and they did not receive any parental love and guidance in their development process. While most of the participants had pursued or continued their education, it might be possible that those continuing their education would have changed their schemas (Beck, 1979). Most of the participants were absorbed into a new education system in the U.S., which could have changed their perception of life. Although loss of educational opportunities and the opportunity to learn the skills for success in life were detrimental, the separation from families might have more profoundly affected the study participants.

Beck (1979) believed that core beliefs are developed and reinforced in childhood to create schemas; families contribute to the development of these. If children are deprived of family in the process of development, positive or negative self-image may be affected (Beck, 2005). The current findings indicated that the participants did not always have a positive self-image, confirming the thoughts of Beck (2005) and Giorgi (2006). Being forcefully removed from families and forced to do tasks the participants might never have done otherwise left a lifelong impression on the participants. For instance, the first participants indicated that her experiences at the camp with male soldiers interfered with her perceptions of men. She was forced to do household chores and forcefully raped on several occasions, and this has interfered with her perception of heterosexual relationships.

The childhood wartime experiences of these now-adult participants and being forcibly removed from their families had an effect on them, their development, and their lives. Some participants wanted to return to Sudan to look for missing family members, but other participants did not want to return at all. That these participants might not have had the opportunity to progress through the typical developmental stages had effects on them in addition to having experiences as child soldiers and life experiences in a war-torn country. All of these findings serve to confirm the findings of Beck and Giorgi, as well as the findings of Bixler (2006), Bok (2003), Dau (2006), Dau and Akech (2010), and Eggers (2006).

At the time of the study, participants were living in South Dakota, a considerable distance from their birth homes in Sudan. Participants immigrated to the United States, but they had been displaced from their homes as child soldiers. Eight of the participants indicated walking distances to refugee camps to escape from the forced role of being child soldiers. They lost families and had to bond with new families in the United States. The lack of consistency in parenting, lack of a home, and lack of parents were all disruptions in the lives of the participants. The U.S. Committee for Refugees (1999) noted that one in five Sudanese people had died because of the civil war. These participants survived; however, their lived experiences have resulted in the possible need for mental health services to address the trauma that they experienced. The report of the U.S. Committee for Refugees indicated a high prevalence of psychological disorders or trauma among Sudanese refugees.

Physical Suffering

Not only was there a disruption of lives and displacement due to the civil war, but participants also recounted numerous incidents of physical abuse, rape, beatings, and pain. For one female participant, being raped led to not wanting to have anything to do with men, including preferring to live with a woman to avoid another rape. Each of the females was raped repeatedly and had psychological scars from the experiences. Traumatic experiences (e.g., rape, physical abuse) involve exposure to a physical or psychological threat, or assault to a person's physical wellbeing, integrity, sense of self, safety, and survival, which have an impact on the person's life (American Psychiatric Association, 2000). The psychological effects of traumas such as rape can have long-term effects (DePrince & Freyd, 2002) or may become associated with PTSD (Scurfield, 1985). The participants in the current study, especially the female participants, were subjected to violence and stress as children or adolescents; the findings of the effects of trauma among current participants confirmed the thinking of Anderson and Spencer (2002) and Beck (1979, 1995) that childhood stress and physical suffering might impact a person for his or her lifetime.

Not only were the females raped repeatedly, but also all the participants were subjected to abuse through beatings, cutting, dragging, nakedness, and having to watch people being shot. One participant stated:

> There were the wounds and the pain, and the worst is fear of losing your life at any time. You hear the shots but you don't know if you are the target. Living in constant fear never knowing what will happen next; who will be the next one to take a bullet, be hit, beaten?

Bixler (2006) noted the children from Sudan have had tumultuous childhoods, and in the process they have sacrificed their mental well-being and ability to function effectively as adults. Physical abuse of different types had left a mark on the study participants, which resulted in (a) grief, (b) depression, (c) physical scars, and (d) former injuries, which were the result of physical abuse during the civil war. Morgos et al. (2008) supported the idea that a large percentage of Sudanese immigrants suffered from psychological symptoms, mental health problems, and possibly PTSD in their current lives.

Hunger was another physical symptom for the current study participants that resulted from the civil war. Rape and physical abuse are one form of violence; living with hunger is another that had effects on the growth and development of both the participants' bodies and brains in crucial developmental years. Participants mentioned (a) always being hungry, (b) never having enough to eat, or (c) being forced to let the regular army eat first and then, if any food was left, the children could eat. One participant recounts:

> Soldiers were expected to be strong with or without food. Most of the times, we did not have food. We slept out in the cold most of times guarding the senior soldiers. The little food that was brought in the camp it was first given to the NMF soldiers.

Aid organizations such as the United Nations did provide succor to refugees, but the participants described walking long distances to reach a refugee camp. If it had not been for the help and assistance of UN personnel, some participants might have died. Some of the participants were left for dead when they became too weak to fight because of a lack of food. They only survived after the U.N. personnel rescued them and took them to a refugee camp. One participant stated:

> Because of the difficult work we were doing at those camps, most of the times we did not have food, and repeated sexual harassment, one I grew so weak, collapsed and I think they damped me. By the time I was regaining my consciousness, I found myself in a track with different people. They were more friendly. Later I came to learn they were U.N. peacekeepers who took me and others to Kenya, at a refugee camp called Kakuma.

Although food security might have been evident before the civil war, participants needed to go farther and farther away to maintain some modicum of food security. Food security in this case means the availability and access to food. Keen and Lee (2006) had described how the lack of food and security, in addition to being detrimental to young and growing bodies, caused stress in the lives of the children. Abdelnour et al. (2008) noted that establishing and managing a refugee community could take years, especially if active conflict persisted. The length of time necessary to establish a refugee community did not allow the participants to receive the type and consistency of food and nourishment needed by growing young bodies. The lack of proper nourishment added stress to the physical as well as cognitive and emotional development of the study participants.

Trauma and Emotional Distress

Current study participants reported exposure to or suffering from trauma throughout their experiences in the Sudanese civil war that continue to affect the participants' present lives well after the occurrence of these events. The diagnosis for acute stress disorder may be applied within the first month after a traumatic event, and the disorder can be characterized as acute when symptoms are present for a period of three months (De Bellis et al., 2010, p. 570). Stress disorder symptoms do not have to appear immediately, but may appear six months or more after an event (De Bellis et al., 2010, p. 570). Trauma such as was experienced and reported by the participants in this study might not have been evidenced until much later in the participants' lives. When the trauma of an emotional distress occurred, the participants were in survival mode, hoping to stay alive. Chronic hunger and sleep deprivation are common in conflict situations and comprised the daily occurrence for study participants. The levels of trauma and emotional distress that participants encountered became a normal experience of daily life. Encountering this level of consistent emotional distress and trauma might have affected these former child soldiers long after the causes of the trauma were no longer present in their lives, and symptoms may not have manifested until long after the trauma had stopped. Several of the participants had difficulty establishing and maintaining relationships, which might result from an inability to trust others as a result of their distressed childhoods. One participant talking about forming new relationships in the U.S. indicated:

> I thought that everybody who saw me saw I was a murderer so I did not want to talk with them and especially tell them about my story as a soldier. The first days

when I came, I did even want to hear anybody say something about my country, I felt like I could hit somebody but I could not because this is not my country [*sic*].

Participants reported instances of having to watch people being killed, including their family members, which was another trauma that could and did have long-term effects on the mental health of the participants. One participant indicated that sleep deprivation and traumatizing thoughts have persisted over the years:

> You know when you cannot sleep because you are thinking about so many things that have happened in the past. I feel like you know what I should have done, I should have allowed the militiamen to kill me instead of me killing people I know. I get traumatized by those thoughts sometimes [*sic*].

According to Magro (2009), when trauma occurs over a long period, it could result in both short- and long-term psychological problems and dysfunction. Evidence of trauma among participants was reported as a painful experience in the minds and memories of the participants resulting in (a) lack of coping skills, (b) lack of positive self-perceptions, (c) memory alterations, and (d) mood alterations, all of which supported Magro's (2009) findings. The participants benefited from different types of therapy to help them deal with their experienced childhood traumas that had carried over to their new lives in the United States. As Gilkinson (2009) noted, participants needed to change their personal schemas or mental images to learn to cope and deal with these experiences. Experiencing trauma at a young age can have an effect on cognition, social skills, physical development, and mental health as shown in the current participants. One participant indicated:

> I am trying to make friends with people of South Dakota, but I don't like talking a lot with them. You know, when somebody does not know what you have gone through, they will ask you questions that will hurt you. So I tell myself, let me leave these people alone, I don't want to feel bad [*sic*].

Life continued to be a challenge for the participants in this study, and although not disruptive or traumatic, might not provide the skills necessary for adaptation to life in a new country and society. One participant describes his experience in the U.S. in the following way:

> Living in the U.S. is better as compared to Sudan and it makes me feel a little more respected since the militia is not here to traumatize us again. However, being jobless, the economic status is almost unbearable. You cannot imagine the bills that I have to pay every end of the month [*sic*].

The American culture is markedly different from Sudanese culture; participants tended to limit their social interactions to other Sudanese because they understood each other better than they understood Americans. Psychotherapy for refugees is not only necessary in dealing with their experiences, but also in working to integrate into a new society and be successful in that society.

The experiences of the individual participants in the study led to childhood trauma and which had lasting effects on their lives. Some of the participants were not able to form or maintain adult relationships. Past experiences were not helpful in participants' search for permanent employment. Differences were shown in how specific childhood traumas affected each individual interviewed for the study. A continuum of influence on the individuals was apparent in which some participants were able to function successfully in most areas of their lives, but had difficulty with the most traumatic aspects of their childhoods. One example of successful overall function, albeit with the resonance of key traumatic experiences, was the female rape victim who only wanted to live with another woman to avoid all contact with men. A number of participants indicated they were participating in therapy, which was beneficial to them in their lives. Therapy might need to continue for the near future as they deal with and recover from the trauma they experienced as children.

Other disorders may also manifest during participants' lives such as depression, anger, aggression, or dissociative disorders (Frueh et al., 2009; Laufer, Brett, & Gallops, 1985). Morgos, Worden, and Gupta (2008) noted that co-morbid disorders might be the result of type, number, and duration of the trauma, which might result in long-term treatment efforts for these individuals. As these survivors of the civil war in Sudan bear physical scars from beatings, hunger, and time in refugee camps for the rest of their lives, so too have the psychological scars of their childhood experiences been apparent.

Every child soldier had a different combination of traumatic events and experiences that resulted in persistent emotional distress. The participants indicated that they still experienced psychological distress many years after the war. One participant indicated that she still experiences suicidal thoughts because of her experiences during the war, especially regarding her experiences with multiple cases of rape. Another participant described constant nightmares because of the war scenes that remained fresh in his memory. According to De Bellis et al. (2010, p. 570), a stress disorder following a traumatic event would be categorized as acute PTSD if the symptoms persist for more than three months after the event. At the time of the interview, the participants were still experiencing symptoms of stress disorders; however, the stress levels were varied based on the kind of treatment that a participant received after the war. For example, one participant stated:

> They take long to settle us in the U.S.. No shelter at that time and me am hungry at most times. They rape me, they beat me, me have my left arm ache due to them beating me . . . those bad militia . . . idiots and beasts. . . . They make me have nightmares in the night, when I see my sister being burnt in my dreams. She scream and scream, I go try and help her but me I wake up and I can't sleep . . . sleepless nights [*sic*].

The presence of these symptoms meant that child soldiers were suffering from trauma many years after participating in the war which had long-term effects on their ability to form healthy relationships. Some of the participants indicated that they had problems trusting people, which is an indication that this lost generation has yet to recover from trauma. Although the participants have been receiving treatment for trauma, they have not managed to overcome the psychological distress associated with their experiences during the war. Even in their adulthood, these survivors of the war still contemplated suicide because of the guilt, shame, and anger that they faced each day. The current findings also were consistent with Roberts et al.'s (2010) findings among Sudanese refugees, which indicated that social, environmental, and biological factors contribute to full-blown trauma.

The participants fled from army camps to refugee camps, but in both places the environmental conditions were harsh. Such environmental conditions could have contributed to trauma among the participants. The Sudanese child soldiers had to adjust to different social settings in the refugee camps and during resettlement in the United States, which was challenging because of the cultural differences. Roberts et al.'s (2010) findings showed that if an individual received immediate treatment after experiencing a traumatic event, such an individual might not suffer from full-blown trauma. The environment of an individual after a traumatic event and other underlying factors such as social and biological factors will determine the speed of recovery from a stress disorder. Unfortunately, most of the child soldiers ran to refugee camps that could not provide for basic needs such as food and comfortable shelter; treatment for stress disorders was even less possible. Although participants reported that life in America was better than life in Sudan, some of the participants look forward to an opportunity to return home and reconnect with their parents.

The participants live with uncertainty about the situation of their family members. One of the major causes of stress disorders in individuals is witnessing the suffering of a significant person (De Bellis et al., 2010, p. 570). From the responses of the participants regarding their families and friends, many of them witnessed their families being tortured by the army. Some of the participants have not seen family members since the war broke out, which may be a major cause of trauma. The constant thought that their family members being dead or miles away from the participants might be a contributing factor for their current psychological problems. Some participants expressed their desires to be reunited with their families, but others were skeptical about going back to Sudan to look for their family members. These participants expressed an uncertainty about their safety in Sudan even though the war ended.

Some participants confessed having persistent negative feelings that started after the traumatizing events from their childhood. The negative feelings in combination with negative environmental, social, and biological factors might have been factors in developing trauma. The traumatizing experiences during the war introduced a new and thinking system for the child soldiers.

The participants indicated that the treatment that they have been receiving in the U.S. for PTSD has been very helpful in their efforts to overcome the long-term effects of the war. Schechter et al. (2007) suggested that treatment for PTSD should incorporate the whole family instead of one individual. Such an approach to PTSD treatment might not work in the case of the lost generation of Sudan because most of the lost boys and girls remain separated from their families. Wesensten and Belenky (2005) suggested that treatment for PTSD should begin with identifying the situational context for each individual. A generalized approach may not be effective because each individual's experiences were unique. In addition, each person is at a different level of recovery. This variation was evident during the interviews in that some participants were comfortable sharing their experiences while others were agitated about their experiences to an extent of almost screaming during the interviews.

Implications for Future Health Treatment

The needs of immigrant survivors of war are many and primarily long-term in nature. Therapy may be a core service provided to the immigrants. However, other coordinated services might be necessary in the areas of (a) education, (b) career counseling, (c) English language acquisition, (d) societal integration, and (e) assistance with learning to manage finances. In addition to mental health counseling/treatment, case managers might need to coordinate resource acquisition with therapy for these individuals to be successful. Study participants and similar individuals surviving war and traumatic experiences need both short- and long-term services.

Counseling might be primary for helping individuals cope not only with previous lives as child soldiers, but also in coping with life during refugee camp stays and dealing with the loss of typical childhood experiences. Before the war, these children had access to education, families, and community support and were growing and developing as might be expected. The long-term effects of being displaced from resources, family, and familiar experience were shown among current study participants.

A need for services for individuals immigrating to a new country exists so immigrants may learn about the new culture and the expectations in a new society. Collaboration and integration of services in different areas is necessary for people to develop a new identity in a new location (Magro, 2009). Before a person moves to a new country, current findings showed that participants would have benefited from education about the new culture and country, as advocated by Magro (2009).

At present, no one single method of treating trauma in war survivors is apparent; treatment needs to be individualized to the person and his or her unique situational needs. Psychotherapy might be used to identify what root causes exist for trauma and to provide treatment for a person to address the traumatic events in order of seriousness rather than all at once. Networking among providers or case managers would ensure coordination of treatment and services for immigrant survivors of war and other traumatic situations. Community volunteers might be enlisted through churches or social organizations to mentor recent immigrants and work with service providers to integrate survivors into American communities.

Specific to the population under study, the lived experiences during the war of the Sudanese lost generation members have been contributors to trauma among these survivors. As survivors of the war, many participants were fortunate to access treatment for trauma, which has helped to reduce the effects of the war on the participants' mental health; however, as adults, the lost boys and girls are far from recovery. According to participants, some of the lost generation members still have vivid memories of war scenes, which have hindered them from living normal lives.

Another need exists to improve access to treatment for the Sudanese living in the U.S. and other parts of the world, including those survivors that were not child soldiers. Noted, effective treatments for trauma such as include EMDR, CBT, pastoral counseling, and art-based therapies could be established in the Sudanese immigrant communities in South Dakota and similar locations. The treatment and therapy sessions should be individualized because each of the Sudanese immigrants is at a different stage of a recovery process. Each immigrant has endured a different combination of traumatizing events.

The study involved the Sudanese immigrants living in South Dakota who have regained opportunities for living better lives, continuing with their educations, and accessing treatment unavailable to other child soldiers who remained in refugee camps and Sudan. It could be assumed that the situation is worse for the child soldiers who remained in Sudan or for those who moved to neighboring countries such as Kenya, Ethiopia, and Uganda. With a living standard in these countries that is lower than the current U.S. living standard, a greater need exists for trauma treatment and therapies for the child soldiers in Sudan and in the neighboring countries. Ending a war and the stabilization of a country after the war does not mean that individual lives are automatically normalized. The narrated experiences of the former lost boys and girls living in South Dakota indicated that the effects of war on individuals could persist for many years and affect their entire lifetimes.

One major factor that hindered the recovery of the Sudanese lost generation was separation from family members. Although some participants indicated awareness that their family members died in the war, others still hoped that their family members were alive and desired to reconnect with them. A practical need exists, therefore, to create a forum or a channel through which the lost generation members may reconnect with family members or determine if family members survived the war. Given the fact that some survivors continue to experience trauma and are unwilling to go back to Sudan, one forum for this reconnection could be conducted online. The U.S. government leaders could collaborate with some governmental and non-governmental authorities in Sudan to establish the whereabouts of the Sudanese people who were alive when the war began. A related effort also must involve the governments of the surroundings nations to which some of the Sudanese migrated during the war. The leaders of these governments might make the data on the Sudanese refugees living in their countries available. If the data is stored in one database, any Sudanese refugee that wished to locate family members could begin to search from the contacts provided in the database.

The Sudanese refugees could not even access food at some refugee camps. The situation at the camps may have contributed to worsening the stress disorders of the refugees. Some Sudanese survivors only managed to access treatment when provided with an opportunity to live in the United States. A need exists for the international community to improve its response to civil wars through assistance to refugee camp personnel to provide for incoming refugees. If the international community is quick in sending aid in areas facing wars, the chances of trauma among the survivors may be reduced. Apart from meeting the physical needs of the refugees, the need exists for counseling and therapy resources as aspects of that aid.

Recommendations

Any research study should give rise to additional questions and suggestions for future research, an approach that is maintained in this study. A longitudinal study over a number of years would be an appropriate follow-up to this study. Beginning the current study when the immigrants arrived in this country would have been ideal, but was not possible. Benefits to other immigrants might result from following refugees from a war zone through the ensuing resettlement for 5 to 10 years to measure (a) how they integrate into American society, (b) how they establish successful lives, and (c) how they deal with the long-term effects of losing so much as children. A longitudinal study could include data on the participants' educational endeavors, work history, and finances, as well as on therapeutic practices.

An additional useful study could be conducted on the different types of therapy that have been used with immigrants and how effective various treatments are in dealing with trauma encountered by these individuals as children. Wars continue to be fought in Africa as well as other parts of the world, and people emigrate from home countries to safer locations. Treatment data could be useful not only with Sudanese refugees, but also with survivors of other wars and traumatic changes. A study on the effectiveness of community resources and integration of services for immigrants would be useful, as immigrants would benefit from integrated services while establishing lives in a new home and country.

The current study population was focused on Sudanese survivors living in South Dakota. Similar studies could be conducted in other geographic areas with different living standards to determine if the Sudanese immigrants living in these areas had similar experiences. Likewise, a study in Sudan and its neighboring countries could be used to establish the experiences of the lost generation members after the war. Such a study would help in determining to what extent individuals who survived the war and still live in Sudan have recovered from the resultant stress disorders. Future research can also focus on other long-term effects of the war in Sudan.

A phenomenological qualitative research method was used in this study. Future researchers could use empirical studies to examine the experiences of the Sudanese lost generation survivors. Future researchers could investigate the most appropriate treatment for Sudanese refugees suffering from trauma and relate it to treatments that could be used for war victims around the world.

Conclusion

A qualitative methodology with a phenomenological lens was used to explore the lives and lived experiences of Sudanese immigrants currently living in South Dakota. The study participants were 10 individuals that had been forced to participate in army activities during the civil war in Sudan. The participants were children when they were taken forcibly from their homes, families, schools, and lives and subjected to traumatic experiences including beatings, killings, rapes, hunger, and the forced viewing of the murders of family or friends by soldiers. Many former child soldiers escaped and managed to get to United Nations' sponsored refugee camps. U.N. peacekeepers worked to place the children in homes in new countries; some were placed in South Dakota. Sudanese refugees faced challenges from childhood traumatic experiences that resulted in nightmares, anxiety, guilt, depression, and trauma. In addition to the natural challenges a person faces in moving from one part of a country to another, being displaced across continents to a different cultural society resulted in even more problems for the participants of the current study. Study participants showed many multifaceted needs; however, therapy and counseling seemed most important for helping the participants cope with experiences and see a new future. These individuals need time and effort in order to integrate into American society and be successful. Time, therapy, and treatment to address their mental health problems from the traumatic childhood experiences will be useful on the way to coping with their previous lives and becoming successful. The lived experiences of the traumatic events encountered by Sudanese children during the civil war were expressed in the current study as shown in the mental health problems, trauma and adaptation challenges of participants. The current study also indicated how community service providers, aid agencies, faith based institutions, and society at large might be of help to refugees in handling the situations of their past-lived experiences.

A one-on-one interview format was used to collect data as participants narrated their experiences during and after the war. Their experiences were categorized into four major themes: (a) disruption of life, (b) physical suffering, and (c) trauma. Only two of the participants indicated voluntary participation in the war; the remaining eight participants were forced to join the army. Participants' education and family lives were disrupted during the war. Participants indicated that it was not possible to continue with primary education in Sudan and only managed to go back to school upon arrival in the United States. The participants were separated from their families, and some witnessed the death of family members. Child soldiers experienced various forms of physical suffering, including torture from senior soldiers, hunger, extreme weather conditions, and walking for long distances. Some of the child soldiers were wounded in the war and witnessed their male counterparts rape the female soldiers repeatedly.

The negative experiences of the child soldiers resulted in trauma. The former child soldiers did not receive any treatment for the trauma and other psychological disorders that resulted from their lived experiences during the war. The participants still bear feelings of guilt, shame, anger, and fear. Some survivors experience nightmares and others have had problems establishing long-term relationships. Some participants indicated that they have contemplated suicide on several occasions. The participants experienced challenges in adjusting to a new life in the United States, such as accessing employment opportunities because of a lack of education.

An uncertainty of the whereabouts and welfare of family members has slowed down the process of healing for many of these Sudanese survivors. Some expressed their desire to return to Sudan and trace family members.

A need was shown to improve the international reaction to conflicts and wars in providing aid to survivors. The poor conditions in refugee camps worsened the stress disorders in war survivors. Government leaders could unite and provide information on the location of survivors of the war. Such information will help the lost generation members trace living family members, which could speed their recovery processes.

Future research might be conducted with an empirical approach instead of the phenomenological approach as used in the current study. Future research may be focused on the experiences of Sudanese in other parts of the world and on the most appropriate manner of addressing trauma for war survivors worldwide.

REFERENCES

Abdelnour, S., Babiker, B., El Jack, A., Wheeler, D., McGrath, S., & Branzei, O. (2008). *Examining enterprise capacity: A participatory social assessment in Darfur and southern Sudan.* New York, NY: Centre for Refugee Studies, York University.

American Psychiatric Association (APA). (2000). *Diagnostic and statistical manual of mental disorders (DSM IVTR)* (4th ed.). Washington, DC: American Psychiatric Association.

Amori, A. (2010). *Risky business: A phenomenological study of how public school administrators experience moral leadership* (Doctoral dissertation, Teachers College, Columbia University). Retrieved from ProQuest Dissertations and Theses. Retrieved from http://search.proquest.com/docview/756360872?accountid=34899

Anderson, E. H., & Spencer, M. H. (2002). Cognitive representations of AIDS: A phenomenological study. In J. W. Creswell (Ed.), *Quantitative research and research design: Choosing among five approaches.* Thousand Oaks, CA: Sage Publications.

Babbie, E., & Benaquisto, L. (2002). *Fundamentals of social research.* Scarborough, UK: Nelson publishers.

Beck, A. (1979). *Cognitive therapy and emotional disorders.* New York, NY: Penguin.

Beck, A. (1999). *Prisoners of hate: The cognitive basis of anger, hostility, and violence.* New York, NY: HarperCollins.

Beck, J. (1995). *Cognitive therapy: Basics and beyond.* New York, NY: Guilford Press.

Beck, J. (2005). *Cognitive therapy for challenging problems: What to do when the basics do not work.* New York, NY: Guilford Press.

Bixler, M. (2006). *The lost boys of Sudan.* Athens, GA: University of Georgia Press.

Blume, S. E. (1990). *Secret survivors: Uncovering incest and its aftereffects in women.* New York, NY: John Wiley & Sons.

Bok, F. (2003). *Escape from slavery.* New York, NY: St. Martin's Griffin.

Braun, V. & Clarke, V. (2006). Using thematic analysis in psychology. *Qualitative Research in Psychology, 3*(2), 77-101.

Brentano, F. (1874). *The concept and purpose of psychology: Psychology from an Empirical Standpoint.* London, UK: Routledge & Kogan.

Brentano, F. (2009). *The Baltic international yearbook of cognition, logic, and communication.* London, UK: Routledge & Kogan. (Originally published in 1874).

Choi, I. (2007). *The lived experience of teachers at a lifelong learning institute: A phenomenological study* (Doctoral dissertation, Pennsylvania State University). Retrieved from http://search. proquest.com/docview/304836387?accountid=34899

Churchill, S. D. (2006). Phenomenological analysis: Impression formation during a clinical assessment interview. In C. T. Fischer (Ed.), *Qualitative research methods for psychologist: Introduction through empirical studies* (pp. 79-110). San Diego, CA: Elsevier.

Creswell, J. (2006). *Qualitative inquiry and research design: Choosing among five traditions* (2nd ed.). Newbury Park, CA: Sage.

Creswell, J. (2007). *Qualitative inquiry & research design: Choosing among five approaches*. Newbury Park, CA: Sage.

Creswell, J. (2009). *Research design: qualitative, quantitative, and mixed methods approaches*. Newbury Park, CA: Sage

Dau, J. B. (2007). *God grew tired of us: A memoir*. Washington, DC: National Geographic.

Dau, J. B., & Akech, M. A. (2010). *Lost boy, lost girl: Escaping civil war in Sudan*. New York, NY: Random House.

De Bellis, M. D., Hooper, S. R., Woolley, D. P., & Shenk, C. E. (2010). Demographic, maltreatment, and neurobiological correlates of TRAUMA symptoms in children and adolescents. *Journal of Pediatric Psychology, 35*(5), 570-577. doi:10.1093/jpepsy/jsp116

De Roos, C., Greenwald, R., de Jongh, A., & Noorthoorn, E. O. (2004). *EMDR versus CBT*. Poster presented at 20th Annual Meeting of the International Society for Traumatic Stress Studies, New Orleans.

DePrince, A. P., & Freyd, J. J. (2002). The harm of trauma: Pathological fear, shattered assumptions, or betrayal? In J. Kauffman (Ed.), *Loss of the assumptive world: A theory of traumatic loss* (pp. 71–82). New York, NY: Brunner-Routledge.

Dixon, L., Browne, K., & Hamilton-Giachritsis, C. (2005). Risk factors of parents abused as children: A meditational analysis of the intergenerational continuity of child maltreatment (Part I). *Journal of Child Psychology and Psychiatry, 46*(1), 47–57.

Edwards, S. (2008). Social breakdown in Darfur. *Forced Migration Review, 31*(1), 23-24.

Eggers, D. (2006). *What is the what: The autobiography of Valentino Achak Deng*. San Francisco, CA: McSweeney's.

Foa, E., Keane, T., & Friedman, M. B. (2000). *Effective Treatments for PTSD*. New York, NY: Guilford Press.

Fox, S. J., & Willis, M. (2009). Initiatory mental health assessments for Dinka and Nuer Refugees from Sudan. *Journal of Immigrant & Refugee Studies, 7*(1), 159-179. doi:10.1080/15562940902935621

Freud, S. L. (1956). Memorandum on the electrical treatment of war neurotics. *International Journal of Psycho-Analysis, 37*(1), 16-18.

Freud, S. L. (2012). A *General Introduction to Psychoanalysis*. (Stanley Hall, Trans.). New York: Horace Liveright Publisher. (Originally published 1920.

Frueh, C., Grubaugh, A., Cusack, K., Kimble, M., Elhai, J., & Knapp, R. (2009). Exposure-based cognitive behavioral treatment of PTSD in adults with schizophrenia or schizoaffective disorder: A pilot study. *Journal of Anxiety Disorders, 23*(5), 665-675. doi:10.1016/j. janxdis.2009.02.005

Gilkinson, L. (2009). *An interpretative phenomenological of refugees' experiences of psychological therapy for trauma.* (Doctoral dissertation). Retrieved from https://uhra.herts.ac.uk/dspace/ bitstream/2299/4470/1/Laura%20Gilkinson%20-%20DClinPsy%20research%20 thesis.pdf

Giorgi, A. A. (2006). Difficulties encountered in the application of phenomenological method in the social sciences. *Análise Psicológica, 24*(3), 353-361. Retrieved from: http://www.ajol. info/index.php/ipjp/article/viewFile/65428/53118

Githens, R. P. (2007). Understanding interpersonal interaction in an online professional development course. *Human Resource Development Quarterly, 5*(11), 253-274. doi:10.1002/ hrdq.1202

Golafshani, N. A. (2003). Understanding reliability and validity in qualitative research. *The Qualitative Report, 8*(1), 597-607.

Griffiths, R. E. (2010). *Developing world.* New York, NY: McGraw-Hill/Dushkin.

Handleman, H. A. (2008). *The challenge of world development.* New York, NY: Prentice Hall.

Heidegger, M. S. (1962). *Being and time.* New York, NY: Harper & Row.

Heidegger, M. S. (1967). *What is a thing?* Chicago, IL: Regnery.

Hodes, M., Jagdev, D., Chandra, N., & Cunniff, A. (2008). Risk and resilience for psychological distress amongst unaccompanied asylum seeking adolescents. *Journal of Child Psychology and Psychiatry, 49*(1), 723–732. doi:10.1111/j.1469-7610.2008.01912.x

Husserl, E. A. (1931). *Ideas: General introduction to pure phenomenology.* New York, NY: Macmillan.

IDMC. (2012).*Global overview 2012: People internally displaced by conflict and violence.* Retrieved from: http://www.unhcr.org/IDMC/IDMC-report.pdf

Isbister, J. A. (2008). *Promises not kept.* New York, NY: Kumerian Press.

Jones, L. L. (2004). *Then they started shooting.* Cambridge, MA: Harvard University Press.

Jordans, M., Komproe, I., Tol, W., & De Jong, J. (2009). Screening for psychosocial distress amongst war-affected children: Cross-cultural construct validity of the CPDS. *Journal of Child Psychology and Psychiatry, 50*(9), 514–523. doi:10.1111/j.1469-7610.2008.02028.x

Karami, G., Ahmadi, K., & Reshadatjoo, F. (2006). Vicarious PTSD in Sardasht chemical warfare victims' offspring. *World Conference on Psychology, Counseling and Guidance, 3*(1), 22-25. doi:10.1016/j.sbspro.2010.07.067

Keen, D. A., & Lee, V. (2006). *Conflict, trade, and the medium-term future of food security in Sudan.* Paper presented at the Khartoum Food Aid Forum. New York, NY: Sage.

Kroch, R. (2009). *Living with military-related posttraumatic stress disorder (PTSD) – A hermeneutic phenomenological study* (Doctoral dissertation, University of Calgary). Retrieved from http://search.proquest.com/docview/304843623?accountid=34899

Laufer, R., Brett, E., & Gallops, M. (1985). Symptom patterns associated with posttraumatic stress disorder among Vietnam veterans exposed to war trauma. *American Journal of Psychiatry, 142*(11), 1304-1311.

Leedy, P. D., & Ormrod, J. E. (2005). *Practical research: Planning and design*. Upper Saddle River, NJ: Prentice Hall.

Luster, T., Qin, D., Bates, L., Johnson, D., & Rana, M. (2009). The lost boys of Sudan: Coping with ambiguous loss and separation from parents. *American Journal of Orthopsychiatry, 79*(2), 203-211. doi:10.1037/a0015559

Luster, T., Saltarelli, A., Rana, M., Qin, D., Bates, L., Burdick, K., & Baird, D. (2009). The experiences of Sudanese unaccompanied minors in foster care. *Journal of Family Psychology, 23*(3), 386-395. doi:10.1037/a0015570

Magro, K. (2009). Building bridges to social inclusion: Researching the experiences and challenges of the lost boys and girls of Sudan community in Winnipeg. *Prairie Metropolis Center Working Paper, 1*(9), 1-14.

Magro, K. D., & Polyzoi, E. (2009). Geographical and psychological terrains of adults from war-affected backgrounds. *Journal of Transformative Education, 7*(2), 85-108. doi:10.1177/1541344609338162

Marchal, R. (2008). The roots of the Darfur conflict and the Chadian Civil War. *Public Culture, 20*(2), 429-437. doi:10.1215/08992363-2008-002

Marlowe, J. L. (2010). Beyond the discourse of trauma: Shifting the focus on Sudanese refugees. *Journal of Refugee Studies, 23*(4), 183-199. doi:10.1093/jrs/feq013

McEvoy, C. D., & LeBrun, E. A. (2010). *Uncertain future: Armed violence in southern Sudan*. Geneva, Switzerland: Small Arms Survey.

Merleau-Ponty, M. (1962). *Phenomenology of perception*. London, UK: Routledge & Kogan.

Moerer-Urdahl, T. A., & Creswell, J. (2004). Using transcendental phenomenology to explore the "ripple effect" in a leadership mentoring program. *International Journal of Qualitative Methods, 3*(2), 1-18. Retrieved from: http://ejournals.library.ualberta.ca/index.php/IJQM/article/view/4470/3594

Morgos, D., Worden, J., & Gupta. L. (2008). Psychosocial effects of war experiences among displaced children in Southern Darfur. *OMEGA, 56*(3), 229-253. doi:10.2190/OM.56.3.b

Moustakas, C. S. (1994). *Phenomenological research methods*. Thousand Oaks, CA: Sage.

Murthy, R. S. (2008). Mental health and psychosocial support in conflict situations in the Eastern Mediterranean Region: Ideals and practice. *Intervention, 6*(1), 239-242.

Natsios, A. D. (2008). Beyond Darfur: Sudan's slide toward civil war. *Foreign Affairs, 87*(3), 1-11.

Okumu, W., & Ikelegbe, A. (2010). *Human insecurity and state crises in Africa*. Pretoria, South Africa: Institute for Security Studies.

Pantuliano, S., & Elhawary, S. (2009). Uncharted territory: Land, conflict, and humanitarian action. *HPG Policy Brief, 39*(1), 1-10.

Patton, M. Q. (2002). *Qualitative research & evaluation methods*. Thousand Oaks, CA: SAGE Publications.

Pizarro, E. (2010). *The lived experience and perceptions of being a distance learner: A phenomenological study of a web-based education program in Latin America* (Doctoral dissertation, New Mexico State University). Retrieved from: http://search.proquest.com/docview/861271490?accountid=34899

Ponterotto, J. G. (2005). Qualitative research in counseling psychology: A primer on research paradigms and philosophy of science. *Journal of Counseling Psychology, 52*(2), 126-136. doi:10.1037/0022-0167.52.2.126

Rahim, F., Abdelmonium, A., & Anwar, M. (2009). Post-traumatic stress disorder in a school in Darfur, Western Sudan. *Sudan Medical Journal, 45*(1), 27-34.

Robbins, B. D., & Parlavecchio, H. (2006). The unwanted exposure of the self: A phenomenological study of embarrassment. *The Humanistic Psychologist, 34(1),* 321-345.

Roberts, B., Damundu, E., Lomoro, O., & Sondorp, E. (2009). Post-conflict mental health needs a cross-sectional survey of trauma, depression, and associated factors in Juba, Southern Sudan. *BMC Psychiatry, 9(1),* 244-254. doi:10.1186/1471-244X-9-7

Roberts, B., Damundu, E., Lomoro, O., & Sondorp, E. (2010). The influence of demographic characteristics, living conditions, and trauma exposure on the overall health of a conflict-affected population in Southern Sudan. *BMC Public Health, 10(1),* 518-527. doi:10.1186/1471-2458-10-518

Rosenthal, R. A. (1991). *Meta-analytic procedures for social research.* Newbury Park, CA: Sage publishers.

Salehyan, I. S. (2008). The externalities of civil strife: Refugees as a source of international conflict. *American Journal of Political Science, 52(1),* 787-801. doi:10.1111/j.1540-5907.2008.00343.x

Salkind, N. J. (2003). *Exploring research.* Upper Saddle River, NJ: Prentice Hall.

Sartre, J. A. (1967). *Words.* London, UK: Hamilton.

Savion, S. (2009). *How do retired military officers start anew in civilian society? A phenomenological study of life transition* (Doctoral dissertation, Human and Organizational Learning). Retrieved from: http://search.proquest.com/docview/288410759?accountid=34899

Schechter, D., Zygmunt, A., Coates, A., Davies, M., & Trabka, K. (2007). Caregiver traumatization adversely impacts young children's mental representations on the MacArthur Story-Stem Battery. *Attachment and Human Development.* 9(3), 187-205. doi:10.1080/14616730701453762

Schnurr, P., Friedman, M., Engel, C., Foa, E., Shea, M., & Chow, B. (2007). Cognitive behavioral therapy for post-traumatic stress disorder in women: A randomized control trial. *The Journal of the American Medical Association, 297*(8), 820-830.

Schurink, W. J., Schurink, E. M., & Poggenpoel, M. (1998). Focus group interviewing and audio-visual methodology in qualitative research. In A. S. De Vos (Ed.), *Research at grass roots, a primer in care professions.* Pretoria, South Africa: Van Schaik.

Scroggins, D. (2004). *Emma's war: Love, betrayal, and death in the Sudan.* London, UK: Harper Perennial.

Scurfield, R. M. (1985). Post-trauma stress assessment and treatment: Overview and formulations. In Figley, C. R. (Ed.), *Trauma and its Wake: The study and treatment of post-traumatic stress disorder* (pp. 219-256). New York, USA: Brurmer/Mazel.

Scurfield, R. S. (2006). Post-Katrina aftermath and helpful interventions on the Mississippi gulf coast. *Traumatology, 12*(2), 104-120. doi:10.1177/1534765606295924

Shanmugaratnam, N. (2008). *Post-War development and the land question in South Sudan*. Paper presented at the International Symposium on Resources Under Stress organized by the Afrasian Centre for Peace and Development, Ryukoku University, Kyoto Japan, 23-24 February 2008.

Snygg, D. S. (1941). The need for a phenomenological system of psychology. *Psychological Review, 48*(5), 404-424. doi:10.1037/h0059710

Sorbo, G. L. (2010): Local violence and international intervention in Sudan. *Review of African Political Economy, 37*(1), 173-186. doi:10.1080/03056244.2010.483890

Todaro, M., & Smith, S. (2009). *Economic Development* (10th ed.). New York, NY: Longman.

U.S. Committee for Refugees (USCR). (1999). *Sudan: Personal stories of Sudan's uprooted people*. Washington, DC: U.S. Committee for Refugees.

Van-Der, B. A. (1996). *The complexity of adaptation to trauma: Traumatic Stress*. New York, NY: The Guilford Press.

Van Manen, M. A. (1990). *Researching lived experience: Human science for an action sensitive pedagogy*. Albany, NY: University of New York Press.

Van Manen, M. A. (2007). Phenomenology of practice. *Phenomenology & Practice, 1*(1), 11-30.

Wesensten, N., & Belenky, G. (2005). Cognitive readiness in network-centric operations. *Parameters, 1*(1), 94-105.

Wild, L., Wild, K., & Han, J. (2008). *International business: The challenges of globalization*. Toronto, Canada: Pearson Publisher.

APPENDIX 1

Qualitative Interview Questions

Q1: How was your life prior to the Sudan conflict?

Q2: Tell me how the conflict transformed your life

Q3: How did it feel to be a soldier in your childhood age, if you were one? How did you become a soldier?

Q4: Tell me about the suffering and physical abuse, if any, you experienced during the conflict. How did that happen?

Q5: Describe any violence you witnessed during the conflict. What was your reaction?

Q6:Tell me of any physical displacement you suffered?
What did you do after that happened?

Q7: How did you leave Sudan?
How did you get to the U.S.?
What was the experience?

Q8: What are the mental or physical challenges, if any, you have faced since you left Sudan? How did it feel?

Q9: How did your sufferings affect your interactions with others and your perception of other communities in Sudan and in South Dakota?

Q10: How does it feel living in the U.S. as compared to living in Sudan? Please explain

Q11: Tell me of any psychological treatment you have received so far here in the U.S.?

Q12: What was your religion prior to the war and was it one of the factors that caused your suffering and displacement in Sudan?
What is your opinion on other religions in South Dakota?

Q13: Have you been able to get new friends in South Dakota and how have you been affected in terms of emotional drain that resulted from losing your friends?

Q14: How have you changed in terms of handling anger and other emotional feelings? Has the counseling been of any help?

Q15: How have you related with those people who are natives in South Dakota? Do you share issues of life with them or do you share with your colleagues from Sudan?

Q16: What was your family life like prior to the war?

Q17: What was your family life like after the war?

Q18: How is your family life now?

APPENDIX 2

Raw Data Transcripts
Qualitative Interview Questions

Participant 1

Participant 1 is a 32-year-old female from the Juba tribe in Sudan. She currently works as an office assistant in one of the accounting firms in South Dakota. She speaks fluently in her mother tongue, but she has also learned to communicate in English while living in the U.S. The participant is one of the child soldiers that managed to survive the war and move to the Kakuma camp in Kenya. She was rescued by U.N. peacekeepers that later assisted her to travel to America. She has managed to complete her secondary education and study office administration while living in America. She lives with her Sudanese foster parents, who moved to America before the war started. The participant does not belong to any specific religion, but she is drawn to Christian faith. This is the dominant religion in South Dakota.

Q1: How was your life prior to the Sudan conflict?

I was still young and used to go to primary school, then come back to play around with children of my age and help in simple household chores such as collecting firewood. Mmmh, also the days I did not go to school I helped my mother at the farm. My father used to work in town.

Q2: Tell me how the conflict transformed your life

I stopped going to school, and got separated with my family. I joined a group of militants and the worst of all, I lost my family. Now I live in a foreign land as a refugee. I feel bad about this.

Q3: How did it feel to be a soldier in your childhood age, if you were one? How did you become a soldier?

When the war started, we did not stop going to school immediately. One day, we were walking home from school with my friends from school. Those were the first first days of the war. We heard a sound from the nearby forest..twaa!! then we saw a track come from the bush and we were forced to get into it by the soldiers who were in it. I was confused because I did not know exactly what was happening. Then after we were dropped somewhere at a camp that had so many soldiers, I knew things were bad.

Q4: Tell me about the suffering and physical abuse, if any, you experienced during the conflict. How did that happen?

At the camp, we were told that we would become children soldiers together with the other boys and girls who were taken there. I wondered now me, how will I become a soldier and what had happened to my country... I almost screamed but one of the soldiers slapped me so hard, I fainted. When I woke up, I found myself guarded by a soldier and one of the girls we had been captured with. Before I could say a word, the soldier told that girl to step away from where I was, and he raped me badly. After that another soldier came and raped me again. I was crying out of pain but they did not want to hear that. When he was finished, he hit me, and then he told me that we shall be cooking for the soldiers.

Q5: Describe any violence you witnessed during the conflict. What was your reaction?

I remember one day, I don't know what had happened, the soldiers went to fight. They came back in the evening and took some of us in the track and drove us to our village. I was thinking that they were taking us home... that was not the case, some the people in our village I think were having a small meeting at our home. When the soldiers saw this, they jumped from the track, and started shooting. I saw that one of the people that had been shot was my father. My mother was seriously injured and she fell down. I do not know if she survived; she was shot at the chest. At that point, I wished I had known how to fight and had a gun... I would have killed these militia men.

Q 6. Tell me of any physical displacement you suffered?

Since the time we were captured, we never had a permanent home. We moved from forest to forest with these soldiers. I had not known this was how life would be like.

What did you do after that happened?

While I was serving as a soldier, I wished I could go home but then I thought, who will I meet because my parents are now dead and I was the only child. In my heart I said, I would learn how to become a good soldier, and then one day, I will kill the soldiers who killed my parents and many more.

Q 7. How did you leave Sudan?

Mmmh I remember that life at the militia camp was not so easy. Those of us who did not do what the soldiers said, they were bitten to death or they were killed through shooting. Those who became weak were damped in the forest or the jungle for wild animals to eat. Because of the difficult work we were doing at those camps, most of the times we did not have food, and repeated sexual harassment, one I grew so weak, collapsed and I think they damped me. By the time I was regaining my consciousness, I found myself in a track with different people. They were more friendly. Later I came to learn they were UN peace keepers who took me and others to Kenya, at a refugee camp called Kakuma.

How did you get to the US?

At the Kakuma, I found other people from our country who had managed to escape the war... every time I listened to them I cried, at night I could not sleep because when I closed my eyes I saw those soldiers who killed my father, and injured my mom badly, even the men who were at the camp, I was thinking they want me to sleep so that they can raped me. Eh, not me again, it is so painful... I was registered by United Nation workers, and then after some time, I think about 1 and a half years, they told me that I was coming to America.

What was the experience?

It was a mixture of feelings of happiness because I was moving to a more peaceful place that I would be sure of getting food, shelter and clothing because we did not have those things at the camp. I also was excited because I would be carried by an aeroplane!! But when I first came to Dakota I felt like a tiny fish that was being chased by a whale. You feel uncomfortable, tense, and worried because you don't know if you are going to make it. Everything is so different and nothing felt familiar when I arrived. I felt alone and frightened. I would like to say that resettlement in any new country is not an instantaneous process. Many refugees thought that their problems would be solved and that the government would provide much more support in terms of financial resources, a nice neighborhood to live in, and good jobs. We were always given the basic necessities by the UN in the refugee camp but now we are expected to be independent.

Q 8 What are the mental or physical challenges, if any, you have faced since you left Sudan?

I know that my parents are dead, sometimes I feel like I want to kill myself...even you, you would feel the same if you saw what I saw. Sometimes I try to sleep I cannot. When I was coming to America I thought things would be okay, but no, I am a refugee..mh

How did it feel?

Some of those who hear that some Sudanese were soldiers they think we are murderers. I do not know if I should live in America or go home...sometimes I wish I were dead, I would not be going through this...

Q 9. How did your sufferings affect your interactions with others and your perception of other communities in Sudan and in South Dakota?

I find it difficult to trust one. The government that was supposed to protect me at Sudan, my father was not there to protect me either when I was kidnapped. Let me just stay with my problems...I really don't know how to talk about my problems especially with the people of South Dakota. Sudanese maybe because we share a history.

Q 10. How does it feel living in the US as compared to living in Sudan? Please explain

If there was no war, I would prefer to live in Sudan especially with my family here but now I don't have a family, if I go back I will be reminded of my past experiences and I am trying to forget. Also in Sudan it is easy to get a good job, it is not like here, I think it is because we are refugees, I don't know.

Q 11: Tell me of any psychological treatment you have received so far here in the US?

We have been going through counselling sessions with the other Sudanese I met here. I think it has helped me a bit, although it is difficult to get over the harrowing experiences that we went through. At least now I can sleep without having those bad dreams. I can also walk outside on my own because I was thinking if I did that, I will be captured again.

Q 12. What was your religion prior to the war and was it one of the factors that caused your suffering and displacement in Sudan?
I did not belong to any specific religion before I came. I was hearing that there was tension between Christians and Muslims... You know the militiamen who captured us were Muslims.

What is your opinion on other religions in South Dakota?
Here in Dakota, I have met Christians. They talk to us on Sunday and tell us to be strong. Sometimes they visit us. We sing, they tell us about God and then we pray. I think they are not very bad.

Q 13. Have you been able to get new friends in South Dakota and how have you been affected in terms of emotional drain that resulted from losing your friends?
I am trying to make friends with people of South Dakota, but I don't like talking a lot with them. You know, when somebody does not know what you have gone through, they will ask you questions that will hurt you. So I tell myself, let me leave these people alone, I don't want to feel bad.

Q 14. How have you changed in terms of handling anger and other emotional feelings? Has the counseling been of any help?
You see, when I was at the camp, I used to see soldiers fighting when they had an argument. Even at the camp, very many boys and girls were fighting; I remember one day I wanted to fight with a boy at the camp. These days, I try to talk, when I cannot, I look at you and cry. I know I am not supposed to fight again.

Q 15. How have you related with those people who are natives in South Dakota? Do you share issues of life with them or do you share with your colleagues from Sudan?
I have friends from Sudan. Those ones, we sometimes talk about our experiences. Sometimes we cry together and then tell each other that maybe one day we might go home to look for our families even if it is the extended family. With the people of Dakota, we have not related with them as much because I am at home most of the time. The only time I am not at home is when I am going for counseling or church. The counselors are not bad.

Q 16. What was your family life like prior to the war?
I can say that we were a happy family. I used to help my mother with the household work and the farm. My father use to bring me something from town and sometimes when he was not very tired, he could help me do my homework.

Q17. What was your family life like after the war?
The day those men captured me took some of us to our village with a lorry; I thought we would finally get back home. Unfortunately, I went to witness the death of my parents. While at Kakuma, I met with one of my cousins who managed to escape. Again, we parted ways because

he remained at the camp while I came here. I do not if we will be reunited again or what... when I came here, I was brought up by foster parents since I was still young.

Q18. How is your family life now?

Right now, I consider my foster parents to be my family... I hope my cousin is still alive. I don't want to get married, I will not be raped again no. but you know, I am afraid of living on my own. I don't know maybe I can find a friend (woman) who I can live with. Men are not very good.

Participant 2

Participant 2 is a 27-year-old male who is married to another Sudanese who has been living in the U.S. A. Both the participant and the wife are from the Juba tribe. They came to America with the help of U.N. peacekeepers from one of the refugee camps in Sudan. The participant is pursuing his college education and works part time jobs to sustain his family. He is a Christian and has been separated from his family since he joined the army. He is comfortable living in the U.S. and is unwilling to go back to his country.

Q1: How was your life prior to the Sudan conflict?

My life, what exactly do you mean... we were living with 2 of my brothers, my sister, and my mother. My father had passed on 5 years before the war, so my mother is the one who used to work hard to make sure that we had food, and any other thing we needed. Sometimes we would help her to do manual work at other people's homes for a pay when we were not in school.

Q2: Tell me how the conflict transformed your life

Now, sometimes you don't know what to say. You see, we were trying very hard with my family to make sure that we have everything that we needed. After the war started, we stopped all this, we lived in fear because we did not know what would happen. We even stopped going to school with. Me and my brothers we would sleep outside to make sure we that provide security for my mother and sister.

Q3: How did it feel to be a soldier in your childhood age, if you were one? How did you become a soldier?

I am the first born in our family. My brothers are twins, and then my sister. So we had heard that if you refused to become a soldier, the National Muslim Front soldiers would kill you or your family members or do both. So when they approached me, I voluntarily joined them hoping that my family would be safe. When we went to the camp, My God, I could not believe what I saw and what I heard. I was so I trembled with fear... We were given guns, we were supposed to go for a shooting training agghrr the shooting objects were us...as in we were to shoot each other, if you successful missed the bullets from the other person you became a fully trained soldier. I remember shooting two of my friends we used to school with... I felt like an animal, I don't know what had become of me...I feel like I want to scream, sorry.

Q4: Tell me about the suffering and physical abuse, if any, you experienced during the conflict. How did that happen?

I qualified as a fully trained soldier. Soldiers were expected to be strong with or without food. Most of the times we did not have food. We slept out in the cold most of times guarding the senior soldiers. The little food, that was brought in the camp, it was first given to the NMF soldiers. When we were going to fight, the lorry that was there only carried the NMF soldiers, us we used to walk for long distances. I remember one day we were walking in the forest, I stepped on a snake. By good luck, it did not bite me so deep and I think it was not poisonous so I survived. Also, we were constantly beaten ruthlessly sometimes without a reason. I think they wanted us to become rough like them.

Q5: Describe any violence you witnessed during the conflict. What was your reaction?
You know, when I joined, I thought my family would be fine. But I was wrong, there was a time me and the other child soldiers were taken to another village next to ours. These soldiers raped women and young girls as we watched. After they finished, they forced us to kill them. I, I, I, I remember I was forced to shoot a lady after they had gang-raped her at gun-point and she was expecting. I knew her... it seemed to me this was a very long nightmare. To bring this nightmare to an end, I thought it was good that I get used to it but anytime I killed, I felt more guilty.

Q 6.Tell me of any physical displacement you suffered?
One day, we passed by our village, I realised that the place was disserted so I could even see any of my family members. For me, I was in the army, we moved from place to place. At times we run away from UN peace keepers to Ethiopia and then came back to Sudan.

What did you do after that happened?
I really wanted to know that my family was fine, so even when we left to Ethiopia I hoped that maybe someday I will meet my family. Sometimes I felt like, these soldiers, I don't know if to kill them or what, they are the reason why I am not with my family. The desire to see my family caused me to gather the courage to escape from my group even though I knew that was very dangerous. I walked for many days alone, In was afraid and 9 days after my escape, I ended up in one of the refugee camps at Sudan.

Q 7. How did you leave Sudan?
When I got to the camp, I was very weak. I met very many people who had left their homes. I met UN workers who put me in their records. I told them where I had come from and what had happened me. At the camp though, there was not so much that was happening. We were so many. The workers were mostly concerned on our security and how we would get food. The days I was there, I would try to go to every side of the camp hoping that I would meet with any of my relatives. I even asked them if they had registered them. I stayed there for 3 months. You know, it is very stressing when you do not know where your family is, you are thinking that everybody knows you killed, and there was constant fear of attack. You do not even know why you are fighting, and why you have to kill. One day, the workers who were helping us came and told me that I would come to America.

How did you get to the US?
It was in the evening and we were very many of us. We were told to get into a bus, then were taken to the airport under heavy security. We went through many places where we were checked and then told to enter the aeroplane.

What was the experience?

I don't know exactly what to say, I was happy to go to a safer place, and I was still thought about my family back at home. Were they fine or had they been killed like I killed other people. I had to continue with my journey though.

Q 8. What are the mental or physical challenges, if any, you have faced since you left Sudan? How did it feel?

You know when you cannot sleep because you are thinking about so many things that have happened in the past. I feel like you know what I should have done, I should have allowed the militia men to kill me instead of me killing people I know. I get traumatized by those thoughts sometimes.

Q 9. How did your sufferings affect your interactions with others and your perception of other communities in Sudan and in South Dakota?

When I joined the soldiers, most of the fighters were from the North, and they forced us to kill our own people. So, me I feel like I don't want to interact with people who are not from my tribe and if you are not, you should be a Christian.

Q 10. How does it feel living in the US as compared to living in Sudan? Please explain

I am thinking living in South Dakota is safer because there is no war. Also you know, even though I would want to go home, I don't want to. I will always feel guilty when I see the family members of the people I killed. Let me stay here. And here, people are very different, in my country; you can never hear a woman talk badly to a man. Women respect men.

Q11: Tell me of any psychological treatment you have received so far here in the US?

When I came, the first thing we that happened was that we were taken through counselling and talking therapy together with others. It has helped me a lot. There was a time I used to think I don't want to live. Now I have changed, and don't want to die quickly.

Q 12. What was your religion prior to the war and was it one of the factors that caused your suffering and displacement in Sudan?

I was a Protestant. I think so, the militia soldiers were Muslims. I think they want to take control of the South, which is mostly inhabited by Christians or they want Christians to convert to Muslims.

What is your opinion on other religions in South Dakota?

In Dakota, there are mostly Christians. I think I like that. If I see other religions like Islam, I will feel bad because of what happened.

Q 13. Have you been able to get new friends in South Dakota and how have you been affected in terms of emotional drain that resulted from losing your friends?

Yeah, I have although it took me a very long time. I thought that everybody who saw me saw I was a murderer so I did not want to talk with them and especially tell them about my story as a soldier. The first days when I came, I did even want to hear anybody say something about my country, I felt like I could hit somebody but I could not because this is not my country.

Q 14. How have you changed in terms of handling anger and other emotional feelings? Has the counseling been of any help?

After my experiences, I found myself tempted to fight whenever there was conflict. The talking therapy I have had with therapist has helped me to get over my past experience and to go back to normal and to accept and also I take medication as well…all the talking therapy plus the medication has changed my life for the best.

Q 15. How have you related with those people who are natives in South Dakota? Do you share issues of life with them or do you share with your colleagues from Sudan?

I appreciate their reception but it is still difficult to open up to them. I prefer talking issues with my fellow Sudanese or the counselors.

Q 16. What was your family life like prior to the war?

I used to live with my brothers, mother and sister. Although we were experiencing financial difficulties, we enjoyed being together. We used to look forward to the evening when we sat around the fireplace and laugh at each other as we shared with each other how each person's day was.

Q17. What was your family life like after the war?

I do not know where my brothers, mother and sister are right now. I hope that maybe that they made it to places like Kakuma in Kenya, or other neighboring counties. If one day we will be united, I will be happy but if otherwise, I have to be strong and move on. When I see families walking together here in Dakota, I miss my family very much.

Q18. How is your family life now?

I am married with two children. I married a woman from Sudan. As I mentioned, the way people treat each other here is very different. And you know, my wife can understand me better because she knows the pain we went through to come here. I don't want my children to experience what I went through. That gives me a reason to want to stay here instead of go home.

Participant 3

Participant 3 is a 30-year-old male, a Dinka by tribe from Sudan. He is married with children and works as an accountant. He lost his family in the war and has no plans of going back to Sudan. Despite the many years that have passed since he escaped from the war, he still suffers from the trauma of having participated in it. He moved to the U.S. with the help of the United Nations High Commissioner for Refugees (UNHCR) and was placed in foster care until he completed his college education. He is still undergoing therapy and counseling for posttraumatic stress disorder and "appreciates their impact on his emotional health".

Q1: How was your life prior to the Sudan conflict?

We use to live in one of the Dinka communities and occasionally visited other towns. My parents afforded us the basic needs such as food, shelter, clothing and education. My mother was a teacher at the school I used to attend, and my father was a business man.

Q2: Tell me how the conflict transformed your life

I grew up in a small village and my job as a young Dinka boy was herding cattle. The civil war in Sudan changed everything. I could no longer take care of my father's animals, no more schooling, and my mother would not go to work also

Q3: How did it feel to be a soldier in your childhood age, if you were one? How did you become a soldier?

When the war broke, we had heard stories of how young men and boys and all or some of their family members were brutally killed for refusing to join the forces and militia groups. So, when one of the militia groups approached me, I voluntarily joined the group so as to save myself and my family. At that point we did not have so much of a choice. You know those stories you read and get scared, and then it happens to you!

Q4: Tell me about the suffering and physical abuse, if any, you experienced during the conflict. How did that happen?

Of course when I joined the militia group I did not know how to use the weapons such as guns. For this reason, I was beaten and severally given death threats if I failed to learn how to use these weapons quickly. In addition to this, we were living in make-shift camps, sometimes we had to go for more than a week without food unless maybe wild fruits, and you were not expected to show signs of weakness or you would be killed. I saw my friends getting killed. I wanted to help but I did not know how.

Q5: Describe any violence you witnessed during the conflict. What was your reaction?

By voluntarily joining the group, I thought my family and I were 'safe'. One day in the evening a few of the militia men took me and accompanied me to my home. They ordered my parents and siblings to all line up outside our house. One of the soldiers held me and two others shot at my parents, my three sisters and my youngest brother while I watched. Also, while in the militia group, I witnessed repeated raping and several cases of kidnapping of young girls and women. You look at those people doing that and you are wondering, this people are beast or what!

Q 6. Tell me of any physical displacement you suffered?

Since the day I joined the militia group, we were always on the run; never had a permanent home apart from the one I knew before my family was wiped out. Later I moved from Sudan to Kenya

What did you do after that happened?

I never wanted to go home; there is nobody to go back to. I felt good in Kakuma Kenya. It was my second home because there was no war.

Q 7. How did you leave Sudan?

Among the militia soldiers, there was a soldier who had been forced to join the group. So, one of the evenings he helped 5 of us escape from the militia camp. We had determined to leave Sudan because we knew if the soldiers saw us they would kills us because we had sworn never to leave the group. We had to cross rivers and walk many kilometres. Some of us drowned when we were crossing the rivers. Fortunately for us one day, a U.N peace keeping track pass by our way they carried us to Kakuma.

How did you get to the US?
I came to Dakota through the help of UNHCR after being at Kakuma refugee camp after 5 years. When we went there, we were registered by the UNHCR workers. They later arranged for us to come to America after so many days of stress, anxiety and worry at the camp. You know we never used to have enough food, and the weather was extreme during the day and night, very hot or very cold because we lived in tents.

What was the experience?
I was relieved that I would no longer have to see the violence and crime committed again. I would not have to fear that we would be attacked at the refugee camp, would not have to go for days without food and water. Life in the refugee camp still affects you regardless of your age and regardless of your ambition. The more you internalize the experience, the more it affects you. I tried to make friends with the older boys and elders in the camp. At night I would listen to the stories that the elders told. They became like our parents. When I think back, I have seen many of my friends die. Looking at the larger picture makes you feel sad, even today. Some people walked 1,000 miles without their shoes. I lost friends who drowned crossing the river. Some people were also shot or kidnapped. Both my parent died in the war. When you become a refugee, you are no longer a citizen. You have to depend on the UN to help you in the camp. I often asked myself: 'Why was life so hard? How could my country do this to me? If my country failed to protect me as an individual, how can I feel proud being Sudanese?

Q 8. What are the mental or physical challenges, if any, you have faced since you left Sudan? How did it feel?
I was still young, and so had to live with foster parents when I came. Living in a family setting, was a constant reminder of the atrocities committed to my parents. At some point I found myself kicking the wall or anything that was close to me. At that point, suicide was an option... I have become a they think I'm a dangerous person and a danger to myself or the others. That was what they were telling me that was the reason behind the section (counseling), me going to section, and uh I felt like a victim, like uh someone uh a criminal being.

Q 9. How did your sufferings affect your interactions with others and your perception of other communities in Sudan and in South Dakota?
Anybody I did know was a suspect. I once trusted strangers (the militia men) and the reward was painful. It did not matter whether you are a Sudanese or not. The only people I trusted a little were people from my tribe; the Dinka.

Q 10. How does it feel living in the US as compared to living in Sudan? Please explain
Living at Dakota is much better. The distance somewhat helps to erase the bad memories, and I have a job though I keep on thinking about home.

Q11: Tell me of any psychological treatment you have received so far here in the US?

The foster parents I lived with enrolled me for a counselling and therapy session especially because of my wild behaviour during the first days. Even at school, we had special sessions for those who came from Sudan.

Q 12. What was your religion prior to the war and was it one of the factors that caused your suffering and displacement in Sudan?

I was a Catholic. I not very sure that religion was the reason but it could have contributed. You know, at the North there are many Muslims and at the South there are many Christians.

What is your opinion on other religions in South Dakota?

Here, there are not very many religions, but there should be no differences between Christians and Muslims.

Q 13. Have you been able to get new friends in South Dakota and how have you been affected in terms of emotional drain that resulted from losing your friends?

It was difficult to make new friends here. I found it easy to make friends with people from Sudan and talk with them. But, I could not stay on my own at school that my foster parents took me. Also at work and the nature of my work, we have to work as team. Sometimes when my colleagues do something that offends me, even unconsciously, it reminds me of home.

Q 14. How have you changed in terms of handling anger and other emotional feelings? Has the counseling been of any help?

The experiences I went through made me vulnerable to anger, fear, bitterness and insecurity. I thought the only way out to solve a conflict was through fighting as I witnessed this constantly during my life at the militia camp, and Kakuma by other children my age, who I later came to know were children soldiers. Since I enrolled for counseling and therapy, I have improved; at least I can sit and discuss issues even though we might not get a solution at that point.

Q 15. How have you related with those people who are natives in South Dakota? Do you share issues of life with them or do you share with your colleagues from Sudan?

You see, you find it easy to relate with people who know you. At first, I was reserved when talking or interacting with the natives. I did not want to talk to them. What made it more difficult is the fact that their culture is very different from us. Although I relate with a few of natives of Dakota well, I prefer to share issues of life with my friends from Sudan.

Q 16. What was your family life like prior to the war?

It was fun going out to herd my father's cattle with other boys at the village. It was fun playing with my brothers and sister. And sometimes my father would take us to visit other towns. You, know the kind of family that you want. I never thought life can change this much.

Q17. What was your family life like after the war?

I lost my family as a result of brutal killings of my direct nuclear family. I do not have the courage to find out the whereabouts of my extended family. Guilt and anger sometimes haunt me. I cannot face any member of my family, because I think they will not understand that everything I did during the war I was forced.

Q18. How is your family life now?

I am married with children. I hope that I will be able to give them the protection I failed to give my family at Sudan. That is my family. I don't want anybody trying to do bad things to my wife and children. I will work hard to protect and educate them.

Participant 4

Participant 4 is a 25-year-old male from the Aweil tribe who left Sudan for Kakuma as an injured soldier. He lived in the camp for a while before UNHCR recruited him as one of their workers and facilitated his travel to the U.S. Since he was used to a different educational system, it was very hard for him to complete his education in the U.S. The war began before he could finish his primary education, and he was forced to join the army as a child soldier. After finishing college, he was unable to secure employment. He could only find temporary jobs but was unemployed at the time of the interview. He has no information of his family, but he intends to go back to Sudan and look for them.

Q1: How was your life prior to the Sudan conflict?

I had a good life with my family. We lived peacefully and everywhere was calm around us because there was no war. There was no drought and everything went on as usual because people traded as usual. Dad was able to provide for family-because he had a job, with everything we needed until the war changed everything. People then begun to become bad neighbours when some people started to preach unfairness in distribution of income, differences between religion and all that.

Q2: Tell me how the conflict transformed your life

Dad used to have a job and support family but not anymore after war begun. At least, even when there were tensions about religion differences and economic differences, parents used to work, so there was no trouble. When war came, it was about minding about how to run away or hide. The war took time to occur, so we never had gone hiding as family. Because you can not predict war even if there are a lot of tensions.

So, we had stayed home because we heard things were tough everywhere else after war. First, everyone minded their live as war went on elsewhere, so he could not go to work and we could not go to school. Within a short while, the war took away everything we had because you could not hold back and die. That single morning we were captured from home by soldiers of National Muslim Front changed everything. Everyone went his/her way. We could not see each other as a family, and I was captured, tortured and made to assist with the war by the brutal soldiers. The focus became how to survive in a brutal war where you could die anytime...from an organized family to nothing like a family.

Q3: How did it feel to be a soldier in your childhood age, if you were one?

Being a soldier was the hardest thing ever because you could die any time. The main focus was not to fight and win but to survive. I did not have the professional tactic or the skill and so it was not simple. Yes, they have trained you but you know that is basic training and you can die with your basic training, so, the rest is yours to learn latter. It is something you never wanted, but must do to live. Not just because someone is watching you to keep fighting but, anytime a bullet could land on you. You face a lot of torture to keep you in the fight. You cannot run away because you know the consequences and the guys are there watching you.

How did you become a soldier?
We were captured from home as I already said. Then they tried to train us to kill people, and that is how we begun fighting. But before were trained they think some will run away or retort, so they beat us up, pierced us with weapons and shot some and we had to accept that there is no running away. So, we accepted and were given guns for training and we start training by shooting people, animals, trees, everything. The training is about one month or so, but sometimes you go to fight before that.

Q4: Tell me about the suffering and physical abuse, if any, you experienced during the conflict. How did that happen?
First, you already suffer when you know the family is no longer with you. After the National Islamic Front soldiers captured me; I still remember the uncountable times I was beaten and you can see the scars all over my body. This was done in an exclusion with any kind of tools they had. That is before we accepted to train as soldiers. They pierce you and threaten you with weapons and beat you up before and even during training. The fear of dying as a soldier then, is something, I think I have to date.

Q5: Describe any violence you witnessed during the conflict.
Yes. I still remember and think about the things I saw from the day I was captured from our house. People fighting, people being killed, cut and dragged naked, tortured with all kinds of weapons. 5 of my colleague children soldiers were forced to kill their own parents and small sisters because of the spying issues and I think I would do the same but it never happened. Every time there are people running injured and bleeding, people with broken legs and arms, some die because someone is denying them food and all that kind of mess. The soldiers also used to capture people from the government and torture them very badly.

What was your reaction?
Mmmh. it was not good and easy to see groups confront each other, children dying and soldiers kill by gun. You want to run away to save your life and you hate these people doing all that. But the point is, you must train because someone is pressing you hard to do it. You cannot try to run away because someone will shoot you from the back or side or forward. Yes, there was a lot of fear as you fight, but you imagine if it was you being shot...so, you hold your gun and shoot before they shoot you. You are in a very bad dilemma and guys want you to fight, else, you die and you don't want to.

Q 6.Tell me of any physical displacement you suffered?
Because of conflicts and war we could not stay away from home. But everything changed when they got us from home because fighting reached where we had. So, they took us but we never saw each other from there. Like the rest of the people, I was always all over running and fighting with soldiers of National Islamic Front as their man, but you train first and it is very difficult. You keep running when you denounce the National Islamic Front because you have an oath they will kill

you when you denounce them. So, you cannot think about it and those guys are very many. I then ended up in Kakuma camp, with lots of injuries, and here am in U.S., several miles from Sudan.

What did you do after that happened?
The only thing I could do in such a war was to run to stay alive, everyday.

Q 7. How did you leave Sudan?
I left Sudan helpless with some other people who were attending to the injured after fighting. They found me with soldiers trying to tie my arm because it was really bleeding a lot. We had already run several miles from where I was injured to survive. I had other injuries all over the body because they beat me up at that point, trying to tell me to wake up and go on with the fight. So, the guys [aid workers] had an ambulance and they were saving life. The solders did not want me to go because they thought I would fight more but I was exhausted and wounded all over. The aid workers gave me some first aid and they drove us to Kakuma in Kenya, together with other fighters who were badly injured after exchange with fire with the government soldiers.

How did you get to the US?
From Kakuma camp, I came, together with some other refugees to US, with assistance from UNHCR.

What was the experience?
It was painful leaving Sudan, with the wounds, but at least we were running from war. Coming to the United States was not really easy because you had to leave your own country, where there were chances of seeing family and relatives. But here is enjoyable and lifetime experience.

Q 8. What are the mental or physical challenges, if any, you have faced since you left Sudan?
The mental challenges are many. You are always stressed because you lost contact with family. No more schooling while at the camp and I did not know about the future. I had lost years for schooling and there are memories about war I don't want to remember anyway. I was shot in the arm and I had to bear all the pain until I was healed.

How did it feel?
Very bad indeed, because this is someone who has messed up with your life and you don't know if it will be back to normal. So, it is a bad feeling. You know you are injured in war and there is someone who shot you, because I was shot in the arm...although those wounds are now things of the past, I can imagine what would have happened if the bullet got anywhere else on my body. There is always that pain coming again and again when I remember.

Q 9. How did your sufferings affect your interactions with others and your perception of other communities in Sudan and in South Dakota?
In Sudan there was no time to catch up with friends and family after conflict, so I was lonely most of the time. In war you cannot relate to anyone. Everyone appears an enemy. Inside the camp, I did not know anyone, which made it impossible to talk about anything. May be we could say a few things we those bringing us food because they wanted us to talk but for me, there was nothing

at all to tell them. At the same time, much time was used to reflect on the actual things that took place, and sometimes others could not live with me easily because we fought and I was rough.

I couldn't take in all that had happened as a very young soldier, and I think it is why I saw the rest as enemies inside the camp. I saw my live totally damaged, and as if the person who damaged it all was right there with me in the camp, so I could get rough anytime. I also felt so bad that someone had made me kill in war and life appeared so different, you know.

Well, I am new in South Dakota, and it will take time to interact with others, although we do talk. Right now, I am slowly recovering from nightmares and thinking about the wrong I did as a soldier-and it is worse thinking about it. I am forgetting things that happened and seeing life from a different angle and I regard them [people in Dakota] as good people.

Q 10. How does it feel living in the US as compared to living in Sudan? Please explain
It feels good and I consider it as a new home altogether. Even though it is hard to trace the rest of the family, at least there is a lot of peace here. Of course there are other issues to care about in life like I am not employed here. There is no one to rely on because my father and mother is not here. Back in Sudan we had good family although it was difficult to unite, we knew there were neighbours somewhere to who you could talk. Now, you do not know your neighbour here. The same feeling you get when you leave a home you are used to; like you are alone. I don't know how they live here and I know it will take some time to adopt.

Q11: Tell me of any psychological treatment you have received so far here in the US?
The people who brought us here have organized some counselling sessions to help us cope with the past. I know it is going to take some time, but I am ready to do anything. You know it is hard remembering what happened and what you saw happen; people being killed, mutilated bodies, bombings and fires and people drowning for fear of death-it is something you don't want to remember but it keeps coming. So they tell us they can help us and we are in it [counselling]. They also bring us medication from time to time to help us [heal].

Q 12. What was your religion prior to the war and was it one of the factors that caused your suffering and displacement in Sudan?
I was Muslim then and I am a Christian now. At least many would know I changed. This is good for me here because many are Christians and I can't imagine the National Islamic Front soldiers, who claimed to be Muslim brothers, did this to fellow Muslim. I was Muslim and I suffered in hands of Muslim, so, it was war and they wanted as to fight Christians, but once you suffer you are no good than those you wanted suffer. Religion differences contributed a lot to war. The fact they tortured us claiming to be Muslim brothers was part of what caused my change to Christianity. The people who preach to us are also Christian, almost everyone here, and I feel I want to associate with them and what they do as Christian.

Regarding cause of war, Ethnicity was also a strong basis for categorization of African vs. Arab), geography (South vs. North), and religion (Christian vs. Muslim) and this categorization caused war, leading to fear, and all problems you imagine about. After war, we feared that categorization would bring new war at camp but at least we survived. Part of the war was, I think, because of differences between South and Northern Sudan, which worsened because of those military dictators working with the government that came into power in 1989, as I heard it with them.

What is your opinion on other religions in South Dakota?
I do think that the war came because of historical differences in religion, being the basis of categorization, so I have some bad attitudes about those who caused this-the Muslims. I feel you cannot claim fighting for a certain religion, yet you punish people of the same religion. I just cannot take that. It is like calling me your brother and you fight me. Yet I feel the need as they say here, to forget everything and forgive-though it is not easy because of family. That is a fact [about family] we must face no matter where we go.

Q 13. Have you been able to get new friends in South Dakota and how have you been affected in terms of emotional drain that resulted from losing your friends?
Yes, I think this is a better home than Sudan, and if family ties were not there, this would be great [home] for me. The people we live with here are a bit receptive and peaceful. They are friendly and we talk to them about who we are, and they tell us who they are. I think with time I can get new friends, yes.

Q 14. How have you changed in terms of handling anger and other emotional feelings?
You see, a lot has changed since I came here, although it is not yet over in terms of handling things from emotional side of view. You know, to remember all what happened, and sometimes you greatly feel like if by committing suicide, you would be away from the painful experiences. Remembering such things brings a lot of hunger and emotions but I don't fight any people anymore, so am peaceful now, you know. Uuh…but you know from the inside right you will not, and with all these efforts.

Has the counseling been of any help?
Yes. First, there was great help at the foster care and counseling, which I was put in because I was only 10 then. At school they also treated us as special people. I think I am coping slowly in terms of thinking about those activities that took place in Sudan, now that am able to reflect on what I can do after life…may be get a job because I don't have one, or do something of value. They tell us about having hope in life all the time and forgetting the past…and I think they are helping a lot. It would be difficult without them because they tell us how we can handle daily things we encounter, like anger, and see others as new neighbors.

Q 15. How have you related with those people who are natives in South Dakota?
Yes I do relate to them nicely like good neighbor. At least we talk about all what happened because people are friendly to us here. They want to know more about us and we want to know more about them, because that is what life is all about. We also talk a lot about this country, issues of work and government too.

Do you share issues of life with them or do you share with your colleagues from Sudan?
Now, I at least can talk to some people, in counseling and other groups, with men who belong here in South Dakota. We also speak about what happened with colleagues from Sudan because they are like my sisters and brothers-that is how I see them. We talk about what we are doing together,

experiences we had as soldiers, how Sudan is like today because we get news from media and we share a lot about personal issues like about our previous families and what happened to them.

Q 16. What was your family life like prior to the war?

Yes. There was a family with Dad and other five children, but not anymore. Prior to war we had a peaceful and good family. We had what we needed. Not very rich, but what you would call a middle class family. There was a lot of love and cooperation from our parents because they took us to school daily, had some days out together; you know the things families do together. Three children of us were schooling and two were still very young. It is painful we cannot see each other now, and may be, not anymore. All the rest are back in Sudan I think, and I fear some are no m

Q17. What was your family life like after the war?

You can say a family running all over if we can call it a family anymore. Think of people running to try and save their lives if I were to judge the rest with my own case. Think of people leaving their property behind because war has erupted near you immediately. Actually, we parted ways the day they entered in our house and captured all of us and we were taken to different places-It is a strategy NMF uses in recruiting soldiers. They keep family members at different places with different soldiers because they are many.

In fighting you cannot have time to search for members of your family…yes, you can keep looking if you can identify family members as you fight, but someone wants you to keep fighting without wasting time. I really do not know where they are now, like I said, and it is hard to say where to start from here, may be get them to here, and some you cannot identify them even if they were alive, and things like that. It is hurting to know it is almost impossible; you cannot return to search for them because the conditions are difficult and there is a lot of fear. I hear people are still in tension back in Sudan, so you keep wondering whether they are alive…but there is always the urge to see them…how? I do not know.

Q18. How is your family life now?

We are separated as I said but I keep hoping they are fine. We are talking about 2 years from now, so it is not long time, you know, but there is no contact at all. For me, am yet to marry, maybe I can have a family in future when I have ability to sustain them…but not now. I am looking for a job, I have good qualifications and hope to get it [family] one day. You know, as responsible person you want to plan where they will live-is it Sudan or not-so, those are issues am yet to be over. Will they keep running like you or not?

Participant 5

Participant 5 is a 28-year-old male from the Wau tribe in Sudan who was working at a cement company at the time of the interview. He is comfortable being away from home because of the peace and a better standard of living. He is single and does not belong to any religion. He is one of the soldiers that sustained serious injuries in the war. The participant managed to complete his secondary education in the U.S.

Q1: How was your life prior to the Sudan conflict?

Although I was young – 14 years, there were no problems in our family. Dad and mum gave us everything we needed because he had a good job. Me and my brothers and sisters lived a happy live, went to school as usual, until all this [war] came. At least then there was no hunger, famine and drought and all hardships I have known to here. It was a young happy life with family where you depend on someone to provide, so, no problem at all.

Q2: Tell me how the conflict transformed your life

First, it is to lose family. It was the worst thing ever, to now. As a family, we basically lost everything, but of the worst was to lose family members. I don't know where they are and it is hard to live with it. Also, because of war, we cannot go to school like we did, it is not possible to enjoy that family life again, and you have to manage it the hard way. You feel like you did many wrong things when young and cannot revert it, it is like you have lost your life while young...no one to watch after you like father and mother and there you are to face life alone.

Q3: How did it feel to be a soldier in your childhood age, if you were one?

I really had to do it willingly no matter how young. It was my teen years and I think I was feeling the energy to fight, so, it did not take long to accept being a soldier when they [soldiers of National Muslim Front] trapped us in school. It is something that would help in the meantime to protect my life, at least as I saw it.

How did you become a soldier?

It was at a school in South Sudan. War had reached where we were and my family had not made any plans to run away because the soldiers messed up all transportation means and you could die anytime when travelling. When they came to school they proposed that we needed to fight to take government and reasons were that things were messed up by government and they wanted to rectify things.

They said government had mistreated, killed people, divided people according to religion and they [National Muslim Front] wanted to put things in order, and I did not see anything wrong with that. First, I thought they were good people with good ideas and almost all were young. We were hearing everything wrong that the government had done, even at home dad used to say these things, so, I supported them at first.

They told us we would be trained peacefully if we accepted to be solders peacefully, but then threatened with all sorts of words about refusing to become one. Some of those who retorted were killed. They told us there was no chance to see our families and that is how some were killed trying to go to their families. There was nothing to do for me but to accept and take the arms. As I saw it, my family would be soldiers too because they never supported the government...at least dad showed us that. I thought may be we would see one another, or they would take us home to see parents because they sounded as good people with fresh ideas. We were taken for training in the forest but first took oath that we would not run away, and then started fighting.

Q4: Tell me about the suffering and physical abuse, if any, you experienced during the conflict.

When you are in training, you don't just get along with things easily. First, we were tortured to accept their way, start killing people and seeing everything as they do. You cannot get in training until they see you have changed and are very bitter so they begin by inflicting pain in you.

How did that happen?

They cut us, pierce us with all manner of weapons and drag us around, naked. Some guys were shot mercilessly as you watch. So, you can't imagine the torture in the hands of National Islamic Front and the need to survive, whether you are in training or not, whether you are already bleeding or fresh, whether you are young or old. There were the wounds and the pain, and worst is fear of losing your life at any time. You hear the shots but you don't know if you are the target.

Q5: Describe any violence you witnessed during the conflict.

I saw people murdered right there by the soldiers and sometimes they forced us to kill youngest ones from our families, sometimes during training because we do not have the skill to shoot. Sometimes we would visit families and the young ones forced to kill their own parents and then captured for training. And, when you join the National Islamic Front they fear some of your family members could be alive and they could be known so, you are forced to kill them.

We saw people die, people being shot, people drowning, people being taken away with broken bodies and legs. Children abandoned and dying and everything is hard to bear with.

What was your reaction?

When I saw all that, it is when I begun having a second thought about the NMF [National Muslim Front] and what they called good ideas. I begun seeing that I had made foolish decision to join killers and if they were killing anyone on their side, then what about me? Although I had joined willingly the army, I had second thoughts about it but now there was no escape route. It is not there at all and the only thing you can afford to do to stay alive is to fight.

I begun having very strong hatred against who were doing this. Seeing that made us continue fighting on to sustain our lives. And by the way, that is all they wanted-to see you with a lot of anger and bitter and so you can fight anyone, I think that is all what they wanted if I look at it now.

Q 6.Tell me of any physical displacement you suffered?

From school in South Sudan we had to run many miles with the National Islamic guys. You see I was young and could not know where we were at any time. All I remember was us getting tied to run when fighting and training. We later managed to run away from the rest of soldiers and they chased us for several miles, left us unconscious after shooting, and some guys dead as I later heard. Some good people then lifted us to Kakuma by car.

What did you do after that happened?

The most important thing was to try and remain alive because you can do nothing about it. You cry in pain, but you must fight, run and run for your life.

Q 7. How did you leave Sudan?

Our home was in South Sudan and as I explained, we run many miles with the National Islamic guys trying to fight people who were actually our brothers and sisters but perceived enemies. Seeing people die everyday even from our camp and the torture, was something I could not take anymore. That was about five months of being forced to do all the wrong things you can imagine in the world. I then tried to escape by running, with many others, after we went into a forest to train how to attack again. I could not know where we were but certainly, several miles away from home, in a forest-that is where they took us for training.

We at first never knew exactly where we were going, but we thought we were at least running from brutal guys...so we thought we would land somewhere. We had run several miles into the forest already and they were running after us. They shot at us and we could not run further, so we were helpless and personally, I was ready for anything that would happen.

You see, you were not running away from soldiers only. It was at night and there were animals and snakes and people were being attacked. I was ready to surrender when they caught us and I thought they would allow us back as soldiers, but I knew there would be trouble because we were breaking the oath, anyway. They shot at us while running after us and beat us up when they caught us. But lucky enough there were aid people who help people during war, I think they were following us. How lucky was that! I heard them talk with soldiers. I also heard them talk when we were travelling inside the ambulance and as they treated us, but could not really know where we were going or where we were. I was in very great pain and I thought it was the NMF guys too, so i feared a lot. So, I was at a very critical condition when leaving Sudan to Kakuma in Kenya, because they beat us up when they found us running away as I explained. Some of us died on the way because they were injured very much by gun shots, as I heard the guys who helped us say at the camp. Finally, I got conscious and was told I was in Kenya Kakuma and many people were there at the camp.

How did you get to the US?

I was assisted, together with my brothers and sisters to get into USA by UNHCR. We came by air. That was about 1 year living in the camp.

What was the experience?

It was not very good because we were completely getting further away from home as I saw it. At least before that, we could think there was possibility of finding relatives somewhere, but now it was getting more impossible as I saw it. I would have wanted to live in Sudan but conditions could not let me, so in one way, I welcomed the idea of lifting us to here. It was the first time I got into a plane even though it was in a very unfortunate situation.

Q 8. What are the mental or physical challenges, if any, you have faced since you left Sudan?

Mental challenges include stress because I keep thinking of the family and relatives...they are nowhere to be seen. It is also hard to think and remember about the happenings in war, the things we did while fighting, and the people we killed. Physical challenges were worse but, of course, there were injuries and pain to deal with.

How did it feel?

Of course you feel very bad about people who did wrong things to you. You think they did wrong by disrupting your life. You are no longer in your home country yet you wanted to live there... there are bad feelings about losing school at young age and the normal life everyone has elsewhere. And you feel you haven't got your life like before war. Even at the camp you don't think peace is possible because NMF guys could come any time.

Q 9. How did your sufferings affect your interactions with others and your perception of other communities in Sudan and in South Dakota?

I feel I cannot relate freely with others if I was taken back because of the fear in Sudan. You do not know who your enemy is. It is difficult here in South Dakota with new neighborhood although it would take time to form new friends. Many times I still want to be alone and reflect about what happened because it still disturbs in mind. It was the same in camp because I was very violent trying to come into terms with everything that happened.

Q 10. How does it feel living in the US as compared to living in Sudan? Please explain

It is peaceful here and better than Sudan. I think with time I will have to adapt. It is not the same as we used [to be in Sudan before conflict] but at least we are safe and can think about our lives together with my brothers and sisters both with new neighbourhoods and the rest of lost boys and girls. You don't think anyone would attack you anytime like back in Sudan.

Q11: Tell me of any psychological treatment you have received so far here in the US?

They have organized counselling sessions we attend, at least to help me and rest of lost boys and girls to cope with the happenings. They are trying to tell us how good it is to forget what happened, even though it takes time I think.

Q 12. What was your religion prior to the war and was it one of the factors that caused your suffering and displacement in Sudan?

No specific religion. The pull between the two major religions in Sudan was major cause of war, yes. We had the National Islamic Front and government emphasizing the differences between Christians and Muslims in North and South Sudan and this contributed a lot to problems. There was also a factor of being Arab and not.

What is your opinion on other religions in South Dakota?

Although am not Christian, I do have very bad feelings against the Islamic people because much of the suffering is associated with the National Islamic Front. First, they tried to show how they would help solve problems caused by government and now they caused all this. That is not acceptable, as I see it now. The only solution is to stay together with peace, no matter what religion you are in.

Q 13. Have you been able to get new friends in South Dakota and how have you been affected in terms of emotional drain that resulted from losing your friends?

I am still a bit fearful because we are new and we don't know people. The only thing we can appreciate is there is peace and knowing where we come from, there is a lot to appreciate. There are new friends from counseling department and school, and I can make more later I think. With counseling sessions, I think they are trying to tell us to adapt and get new friends and see life more positively. It is difficult having lost friends we used to be with as children and you don't know how to make more.

Q 14. How have you changed in terms of handling anger and other emotional feelings? Has the counseling been of any help?

Sometimes it was difficult in camp because I could fight people. Staying with them was hard because I had a lot of pain and anger. I saw them as enemies. Many feared and avoided me, but I think there is change. At least I can talk to my sisters and brothers from South Sudan who we came with and can take it easy. Sometimes I felt like suicide would be better to relieve the pain and memories of bad things I did. That was at the camp, but I think things have changed now with counseling.

Q 15. How have you related with those people who are natives in South Dakota?

We share issues with colleagues from South Sudan and also some from Dakota. We talk about our history to them and they tell us who they are. They keep visiting us and hearing our stories, so they are good buddies here. I think they are good neighbors, although it will take time to talk to all. I have friend from the counseling group who live here and I think we talk about those issues.

Do you share issues of life with them or do you share with your colleagues from Sudan?

Yes we do share a lot of issues, both personal or not. We talk about what happened to us in Sudan, at the camp, and what our families went through. We meet and share things together and they are friends, even though we come from different places back in Sudan.

Q 16. What was your family life like prior to the war?

As I mentioned we had a good family and were living normal and happy lives in North Sudan before fighting, like anyone else. I used to go to school, but after war, I could not manage. At the camp, they tried yes, and I got back to school of which I appreciate because I have a job with a cement company to sustain me. It is a good job based on my qualifications at technical school.

Q17. What was your family life like after the war?

Tattered family because we could not, and even now, we cannot see each other. I don't know if they became soldiers or became killed or anything like that. It was running for life for everyone, some died but me survived. I still do not know how many died. I left to the camp alone from the family and so, I could not know. It is hard not to see them although you feel you would like to.

Q18. How is your family life now?

I do not have a family. I do not know because it is difficult to find my father, mother and other 5 sisters and brothers. You even do not know if they are alive. I am yet to get married, but may be one day after a while. I can have my family. I want my family to live a good live as we lived or better than that before war in Sudan, and more to that, without threat of war.

Participant 6

Participant 6 is a 24-year-old male from the Aweil tribe. Since he moved to the U.S., he has only managed to complete his secondary education and thus has no professional skills. Lack of education has limited his ability to access formal employment. He was a violent teenager who could not get along with his foster parents, and he is now living alone in South Dakota. Their disagreements limited his chances of accessing higher education.

Q1: How was your life prior to the Sudan conflict?

I had a family and we lived a very comfortable life at North of Sudan. We had everything we needed and never knew it would be this later. Life was good, no drought or famine when with parents and other members of the family.

Q2: Tell me how the conflict transformed your life

It changed every bit of our lives, family life and all the comfort we had was taken away from us. No one could work because of the differences of people and drought came in. I think it changed all things with the mental changes and separation. It is not easy to take in. I had better chances to get education, good education, but that is lost and completely lost.

Q3: How did it feel to be a soldier in your childhood age, if you were one? How did you become a soldier?

It was so bad I do not like remembering all that. Uhh! I was forced after kidnapping from school as a young boy of 12 years and I was so badly injured by the soldiers and almost died and could not progress with war and fighting. First, the rough guys from NMF [National Muslim Front] wanted to train us. First, they made us take oath that we cannot run away and if so, we be killed. We could not fight without skill and first is training, but at least I got a chance and was taken away at bad situation.

Q4: Tell me about the suffering and physical abuse, if any, you experienced during the conflict.

There was torture at the NMF camps because they wanted us to assist. You don't just agree to do that and they have to beat you up, and my body has a lot of scars. Well, that is things behind us now because the physical abuse [wounds] are healed now, but you see it is hard to forget it. Some of children were forced to sometimes shoot people before training to be shown how to do it because we never knew that [to shoot], and many died. Sometimes I dream about all that, I cry about it and wail a lot. It was and still hard to take it in [accept].

How did that happen?

The National Muslim Front hurt anyone. They exclude you to a secret location, they beat you seriously, and then they give you an oath before training. Of course, the mental issues of being without a family happen because we are not together anymore. They hurt you because they want you to keep fighting for them.

Q5: Describe any violence you witnessed during the conflict. What was your reaction?

A lot of people dying, people being shot, people being bullied and cut into pieces alive...all that. You think you will be the next one on the line, but you must do everything to live. Sometimes we went into forests and people are attacked by snakes and they die. It was painful a lot but it made people run faster for their lives. But for me, it made me more fearful and fight more for my live.

Q 6. Tell me of any physical displacement you suffered?

It had to be getting out of home area through kidnapping from school. I never returned home. I did not want to live or to fight...it was not my choice. Those soldiers of NMF pulled us forcefully and at gun point and we took oath. But I also ended at Kakuma, in very worse situation, and at this point you are feeling like death or even suicide would be much better to relieve you of the happenings.

What did you do after that happened?

I ended in Kakuma and I just had to stand up [take courage]. At least you have to think about living, no matter what. After the displacement, I could not go anywhere. I just stayed at the camp because there were a lot of tension still in Sudan, South or North. At least I regarded camp as peaceful. But while in war we run several miles with soldiers and the only thing I could do in such a war was to run to stay alive, everyday.

Q 7. How did you leave Sudan?

After capturing by the NMF and all that torture, I became exhausted at one point and got hurt. You know tiring up and you still see people fighting. I had to do something as I remember and that was to run away. At this time [point], I was injured and there was no progressing with anything and I got trapped between soldiers and aid guys. Of course there was the beating and everything like that but worst of it was the shot on the foot as we fought soldiers from the government side. Yes, the soldiers said they had trained me as their own so they cannot let me go I would rather die, but the aid workers wanted to lift me away and assist me. At last the aid workers worn and they took me to Kakuma in Kenya.

The NMF had left me helpless because they were running away from other soldiers. And those people giving aid to injured in war picked us from there. They drove us to Kakuma in Kenya. I was in great pain but they attended at our injuries at least. I could hear us move but I never knew where we were, so it was that bad.

How did you get to the US?

From Kakuma we came [with] a number of guys through [by] plane here in South Dakota.

What was the experience?

There was the feeling that by going further away to Sudan, I would have no chances of getting family members, so I wanted to stay...but there were important things to see ahead [look at], like having a good life later. It was hard to accept because of that [thinking about family], but at last I came as a member of lost boys and girls.

Q 8. What are the mental or physical challenges, if any, you have faced since you left Sudan?

No physical challenges but mental include stress about family members...you know getting to think whether they even are alive. It is difficult to take it and you know even it can't be possible to see them...uh! tough. You don't know how many could be dead and there is no talking to them. You also still remember what happened and ask why all that.

How did it feel?

Very painful and hard for me. Yes. I can't imagine. Very hurting to know that your life was OK, but someone just destroyed it. You cannot return back to have a family you just had. There is no way you can take that [accept]. Sometimes I felt hopeless and uncomfortable thinking about my family and it was tricky associating with new people.

Q 9. How did your sufferings affect your interactions with others and your perception of other communities in Sudan and in South Dakota?

I feel bad about those who did all this. Those who NMF who did this to us and their army guys. For the communities may be it is still Sudan and your home country, but there are those who did wrong-not everybody. South Dakota is a new home me and the rest from Sudan need to adapt to, you know talk to others [associate] and move on with our lives. I mostly use time alone to reflect about what happened and fear to associate with everyone is still in [me], but we talk as lost boys and girls or with anyone because at least it is safe and no war. In Sudan you could fear anyone because you do not know what they think about you.

Q 10. How does it feel living in the US as compared to living in Sudan? Please explain

US is peaceful, so no much problem like Sudan. The best thing you can get is peace, anywhere. There is no fear of being killed by gun or tortured like Sudan, although it [South Dakota] is a new home. At least here you don't fear people may attack you anytime.

Q11: Tell me of any psychological treatment you have received so far here in the US?

They have been talking to us in the sessions [counselling] and from time to time. Yah, about forgetting what happened and dealing with all emotions we have about it.

Q 12. What was your religion prior to the war and was it one of the factors that caused your suffering and displacement in Sudan?

Christian. The war was because some were Muslims and others Christians and that affected a lot. Although there was the issue of some being Arab fighting Africans but you know most Arabs have Muslim beliefs so is about religion. NMF [National Muslim Front] is itself Muslim. There was also the changing of education into Arabic language and system and people could not agree, which shows religion issues there.

What is your opinion on other religions in South Dakota?

The fighting about religion has no point and the Muslim NMF did not need to do that [cause chaos]. I don't think religion should cause all that problems.

The National Muslim Front had no point at all to claim trying to rectify what the government had done, yet it tortured even people who fought for it. I do not think I have anything negative about any religion, but you see it is nothing trying to fight with people of a given religion. It is unacceptable to think that a religion can cause all such troubles.

Q 13. Have you been able to get new friends in South Dakota and how have you been affected in terms of emotional drain that resulted from losing your friends?
Yes, we are adapting. There are friends in the counseling department and those who visit us from time to time…we talk. Both with my fellow Sudan guys [fellow refugees] and people here. Yah, it has something to do with seeing life differently in a new environment and one of them is to make new friends and see everything.

First, there are those guys [counseling] trying to let us see life in a different way, yah. And you feel they have a point because they are helping build your life again. So, they tell us to create new friends and see life differently.

Q 14. How have you changed in terms of handling anger and other emotional feelings?
Yes. It is slowly getting back to normal…but as they say and as I can see, it is going to be fine. I have hope a lot. I don't fight any more with anyone like it was in camp when I would see everyone as enemy because of pressure [emotional stress] thinking about what their [MNF] soldier did to me and my life.

If you think of the time we were in the camp, there were times I was not friendly at all to the people there. I think because I had bad feelings about what had happened in Sudan. But I think I would not do that if I went back there. I don't see people here as enemies and I have positive view of life.

Has the counseling been of any help?
Yes, a lot. Because we have learnt how to reduce those emotional reactions because of what happened. I think the ability to create new friends and see others as friends by default comes because of the healing through counseling. They are showing us how to eliminate negative thoughts because of what happened, deal with the past and start a new life. I think they have helped me deal with the tensions in my mind about what happened.

Q 15. How have you related with those people who are natives in South Dakota?
Yes, very well and we talk about what happened, both with people hear and those we came with, who are from Sudan. We share a lot with them [fellow Sudanese] and we talk about it [what happened] big times [a lot]. They want to here us and they listen to our stories and we also want to know what happens in their life.

Do you share issues of life with them or do you share with your colleagues from Sudan?
We also speak about what happened with colleagues from Sudan because they are my sisters and brothers. We talk of what happened back at home country Sudan, what we can do in future, and we consider each other as brothers and sisters, now that we are in a new country. It helps us to see that really, the problem was not anyone of us, but those who instigated violence in South Sudan. We talk about issues to do with families we had and experiences we had at young life, and all things like that.

Q 16. What was your family life like prior to the war?
Mmmh! As I mentioned there was Dad, mum and three children in our family, with a lot of things and property, but a lot has changed since fighting days [war in Sudan]. There is no…uh..

family, no communication and you don't know what the rest saw [what happened to the rest]. I would very much like to meet them but I don't know how. It is hard to adjust about family, with no hope of seeing them again.

Q17. What was your family life like after the war?
There is no one to see the other [as family] and you cannot say where they are. You see they also do not know whether I am here even…they don't and it is hard for them I know, if they happen to be there [alive]. Now we are called lost boys and girls because our families are lost and disrupted because of war.

Q18. How is your family life now?
For the rest of the guys, I just don't know. It is everyone [family members] running and may be, we may not meet. I do not know. I hope we can meet one day. I don't have a family myself. May be latter when I am married. It is hard because you need to support them if you can get a job. I didn't manage to finish school and no specific training, no good grammar but I hope to get a casual job that I can help myself and family if it will be there in future.

Participant 7
Participant 7 is a 26-year-old woman living with her husband in South Dakota. She has no formal education, and she is still learning English as a second language. She is from the Dinka tribe in Sudan. She cannot find work due to lack of education. She does not belong to any particular religion and has no knowledge of the location of her family. She is among the Sudanese who had a rough time in the U.S. due to a lack of a basic education and a stable source of income. Her foster parents separated, and she had to live on the streets.

Q1: How was your life prior to the Sudan conflict?
My parents keep fighting every day and eventually they divorced, we ended up living with my mother, we are suffering because we have no enough food. Me I kept dropping out of school for lack of school fees. My clothes were torn and some of my friends laugh at us but some were very warm and gave us food sometimes…but my mother love all of us and we love all of us, us never fought and we had peace…me I wish those days never changed

Q2: Tell me how the conflict transformed your life
Us we spent many days in the forest and hunted for wild animals and fruits. You know sometimes, we were bitten by some insects and it was painful. Unfortunately, our three-month-old baby died of hunger. My sister too was killed. Me I get angry and frightened very fast and I had to go through the psychological trauma and life is no longer the same.

Q3: How did it feel to be a soldier in your childhood age, if you were one? How did you become a soldier?
I felt undermined, rejected and angry…why do they have to come interrupt my education? Me, I don't enjoy being a teenage girl who had the attention from the young boys. They steal my youth and my dignity. They came to our school one day and take us as a group. They beat everyone who tried to ran away. They take my hands and tie me and then, the next minute I become a child soldier. They are idiots

Q4: Tell me about the suffering and physical abuse, if any, you experienced during the conflict. How did that happen?

They beat me, they rape me, seven of them.... they are beasts, beasts and nothing more. They make me wash their clothes and made me tie their wounds. Sometimes me want to hit their wounds and run away.....but what if they catch up with me? They would kill me..... me cry every day I remember.

Q5: Describe any violence you witnessed during the conflict. What was your reaction?

They come, they burn many of my friends alive. They are no people, they are beasts for lack of no better word...my sister, me watch her burn t alive, why? Why? Why? Me wish it was just a bad nightmare but no. I scream and scream from a distance and then some militia tell me to shut up and they tell me to go and cook for him, because I am his wife. I fainted I don't know what happened after that, the next day, I find myself in the camp, tied.....

Q 6.Tell me of any physical displacement you suffered?

At war break, we are displaced from our home at Sudan, me and my other siblings then we are took to Ethiopia. Us walked many miles with no food, no water. We travelled as a group ranging from 17,000 to 25, 000 refugees from Ethiopia to Kakuma refugee camp. Sad thing, only less than 11,000 Sudanese, we arrived at Kakuma.

What did you do after that happened?

Life at Kakuma refugee camp, no enough food, we fight to get little food. Me just seat and remember all...me get very sick with fatigue, and malaria, because of the diverse weather change

Q 7. How did you leave Sudan?

We leave, me and other of my friends from Sudan as a group of thousands and us we walked for many miles to Kenya. .... the most tiresome and dangerous experience I know about. We were exposed to treacherous rivers, wild animals especially snakes and lack of food and water. Me i remember one day, I almost drowned as I try cross a big river, but my friend Andrew save my own life...the only good thing is that we get to Kenya at Kakuma refugee camp somehow.

How did you get to the US?

The UNHCR made it happen for us. I am happy they come one day to Kenya, take us from Kenya, and taken us to the U.S

What was the experience?

They have many different refugees, who are different from me and have linguistic, cultural and ethnic differences. Hard to talk and interact to them and tell them what I want and think about something. Me I feel lonely and misunderstood not to mention that I do not have my family with me all this time since we left Sudan

Q 8. What are the mental or physical challenges, if any, you have faced since you left Sudan?

They take long to settle us in the US. No shelter at that time and me am hungry at most times. They rape me, they beat me, me have my left arm ache due to them beating me....those bad militia...idiots and beasts.... They make me have nightmares in the night, when I see my sister being burnt in my dreams. She scream and scream, I go try and help her but me I wake up and I can't sleep......Sleepless nights....

How did it feel?

I feel I want to kill them....if me I know who they are and where, me I would go and kill them.. all those who raped me and burn my sister alive. Angry with the militia, guilty for not saving my sister...ooooh my sister, me I feel just hopeless that I would not change this situation

Q 9. How did your sufferings affect your interactions with others and your perception of other communities in Sudan and in South Dakota?

I got angry easily since I was bitter. Me I never trusted anyone regardless of who he or she was. Me I viewed other communities in Sudan and South Dakota as my rivals.

Q 10. How does it feel living in the US as compared to living in Sudan? Please explain

Life in US as me being woman is not as discriminating in terms of gender as in Sudan. I feel more peaceful and secure than in Sudan. However, the bills notwithstanding, I am not employed as am expecting my first baby....o my baby, my first and only baby, has brought me joy and happiness and me can smile again but now, these bills in the US are very high to cope with

Q11: Tell me of any psychological treatment you have received so far here in the US?

That doctor treated me for PTSD (Post-traumatic stress order) due to chronic stress. I also go and attended counselling sessions.

Q 12. What was your religion prior to the war and was it one of the factors that caused your suffering and displacement in Sudan?

Me did not have any religion. It partially contributed to my suffering ...you see, I was not among the Christians and then, the Christians discriminated the Muslims... you know, Christianity was the only recognized religion

What is your opinion on other religions in South Dakota?

I disliked all of them, that it why you see, I never got committed to any.

Q 13. Have you been able to get new friends in South Dakota and how have you been affected in terms of emotional drain that resulted from losing your friends?

I have very few friends in South Dakota most of them I meet them recently through my husband[....yes I am married now!] you know, I have not yet been able to heal emotionally from the loss of my sibling and friends who died in the war. This has made me withdrawn and anti-social for long

Q 14. How have you changed in terms of handling anger and other emotional feelings? Has the counseling been of any help?

I must say that the counseling they give me has been of great help to me. Me I was so afraid to meet strangers like you, but that has reduced by the day. However, me get angry very fast but with the counseling, I am able to manage it effectively. You see, like when you tell me to answer these questions and then me I tell you I want to go home and cook for my husband and then you tell me…please it will not take long…then me at first I get angry and I want to tell you to leave me alone or I will beat you.. Then I seat and just decide to fill the questions…

Q 15. How have you related with those people who are natives in South Dakota? Do you share issues of life with them or do you share with your colleagues from Sudan?

I talk to the natives in South Dakota with ease in the recent days since my husband they talk with them but it was not at the begging. In accord to my cultural backgrounds, me I just share my life issues with my fellow Sudanese.

Q 16. What was your family life like prior to the war?

My parents were separated because my dad beat mum and mum tell dad bad words. We lived with my mother and the rest of my siblings. We were poor and hardly hard enough food but we all loved each other.…

Q17. What was your family life like after the war?

My two sisters die in tragic circumstances so we are minus one, the emotional drain was too much. Me I cry and cry. Me I hate the ones that kill my sister. We are only two siblings left. We never found our parents again after the war. They must have been killed as well.…

Q18. How is your family life now?

We are very close with my other sibling, my wonderful brother and the wonderful news is that I me I meet the most handsome man and me am married now, and expecting my first baby!

Participant 8

Participant 8 is a 29-year-old male who was working temporary job at the time of the interview. The participant is one of Sudanese who managed to reunite with their families after the war. His family travelled to the U.S. soon after he travelled as a UNHCR worker. He has not managed to complete his college education due to a lack of finances, and he has to support his family as well. He is a Muslim, and he partly blames his religious background for both the suffering he experienced in Sudan and his unemployment in the U.S. He is from the Juba tribe in Sudan.

Q1: How was your life prior to the Sudan conflict?

The truth is, am not gonna say, us we have the luxury we needed when we lived in Wau land, but we had the basic needs. My siblings and me attended school and afforded good food. I spent some of my time attending to our flock. We had many friends and life was peaceful.

Q2: Tell me how the conflict transformed your life

The militia, they interrupted my education and I lost my dream of being a successful lawyer to it. I am heartless I do not feel mercy to any one, because even them, the militia they do hurtles thing to us.

Q3: How did it feel to be a soldier in your childhood age, if you were one? How did you become a soldier?

They take us with my friends when us we are grazing my father's cattle and playing. Then they beat us and force us to enter in their track. They take me to be a soldier. Me I feel very not respected and useless. They make me feel guilty because they force me kill my own father... oooooooohhh....me I just feel to kill myself many times when I remember how they did it....

Q4: Tell me about the suffering and physical abuse, if any, you experienced during the conflict. How did that happen?

Us we hide from the militia as a group. However, one day as we hide in the forest, some of the militia caught up with us and beat us up mercilessly before kidnapping my friends. I was unconscious and they probably left me because they thought I was going to die. One my friends found me. I was subjected to treatment, which now saw me recover only that the trauma is still there...but you see, later they take me and make me to be a child soldier

Q5: Describe any violence you witnessed during the conflict. What was your reaction?

They make me shoot my father....me still can't explain about it because I have no words...but on that day, father told me not to feel guilty because it was not me and he tell me to shoot him so that they not kill both me and him. Him choose to die alone...me miss him...Me I have never been the same...I did not cry, because it was beyond the point of me crying... but me just faint after I see him on the floor with blood....

Q 6.Tell me of any physical displacement you suffered?

Us we are were displaced within Sudan for more than five times. Unfortunately, many of my friends died on the way due to lack of food, wild animals and drowning. My best friend drowned in the river, he was calling out for me to help him.....me still remember how he called me and me wouldn't help him

What did you do after that happened?

We did not have shelter, me I did not have my family anymore. The saddest is, me was I witnessed widespread burning and killings and worst of it all, it was continuous

Q 7. How did you leave Sudan?

I and many of my friends we say to ourselves, we will die here let us run away....so you see, we walked from Sudan to Kenya where us camped at Kakuma refugee camp. It took us many days and many of my friends died on the way. I was lucky to make it to the camp

How did you get to the US?

Me I say, I credit the UNHCR for relocating us from Kakuma refugee camp in Kenya to the United States.

What was the experience?

You see, it is very hard to adapt to the new social, cultural, legal and religious systems. I was emotionally strained since I had been separated from my family, relatives and friends for a long period. It was a traumatizing experience.

Q 8. What are the mental or physical challenges, if any, you have faced since you left Sudan?

I knew I needed help but I did not have the confidence to ask for it. I wondered What picture are they gonna have of me, you know when they [say], well he's in contact with PTSD and he's getting help and PTSD is a place that you need help if you are affected by trauma by let's put it this way, something scary, and doesn't that make you like a scary cat or something ... you don't want to produce something that position, you don't want to see yourself like that". It was a predominant challenges I faced since I left Sudan.

How did it feel?

Me you know, I suffered chronicle stress, trauma and emotional stress. You don't know how I feel after I remember my father is lying on the floor because me I shoot him... many times I feel suicidal and many times me I am very angry and guilty

Q 9. How did your sufferings affect your interactions with others and your perception of other communities in Sudan and in South Dakota?

From the first, I was bitter with everyone including myself and I would not talk to any one for fear of being hurt. I say I have nothing against them even though they are not my favourites.
Q 10. How does it feel living in the US as compared to living in Sudan? Please explain
Living in the US I tell you I feel more secure and peaceful since we do not have the militia pursuing us. However, I will tell you this; one of the most challenging factors is rent and hospital bills. Unemployment...imagine me look for employment they don't give me employment because me I am a Muslim and us we are discriminated from our Christian friends.

Q11: Tell me of any psychological treatment you have received so far here in the US?

They give me counselling sessions. Also, me I received PTSD (Post-traumatic stress disorder) treatment.

Q 12. What was your religion prior to the war and was it one of the factors that caused your suffering and displacement in Sudan?

Me I was Muslim. It contributed greatly to my suffering and displacement in Sudan. They ask me are you Muslim or Christian even though they see me I am dressed up like a Muslim and then I say Muslim...they land me a slap.......They never recognize us as Muslims.

What is your opinion on other religions in South Dakota?

I tell you me never ever like them.....you see, they discriminated us.
Q 13. Have you been able to get new friends in South Dakota and how have you been affected in terms of emotional drain that resulted from losing your friends?
I have very few friends in South Dakota. I still mourn over my friends and that has made my chances of making new friends limited.

Q 14. How have you changed in terms of handling anger and other emotional feelings? Has the counseling been of any help?

This counseling help me but in a small percentage. Am still angry and it is hard for me to manage my anger. I say am angry just like that

Before I'm coming to therapy I was thinking about the ... other world and I was thinking how can I just umm just comfort myself, what can I do to something for myself, it looks like that he has been thinking about as he says has been thinking about how he can suicide or something like that".

Q 15. How have you related with those people who are natives in South Dakota? Do you share issues of life with them or do you share with your colleagues from Sudan?

I relate to natives in South Dakota in a cold approach…..you see, me I have barely healed emotionally. I share my issues with my colleagues from Sudan… you see I do not trust the others.

Q 16. What was your family life like prior to the war?

My family was great….imagine us we live together as one. Me I wish that those days come back

Q17. What was your family life like after the war?

With the death of my father, I was left alone with my mother and sister. However, it was my pleasure to have them with me. I see my mother and me run to her…then us we are crying to see each other because me I love her..very much and then my sister…she is our little angel… even though dad leave us, we are happy to have each other… they make me have reason to live tomorrow…

Q18. How is your family life now?

I am not married but you see me I meet this girl. Before I am meeting her me I wish to have a fiancée and then I am meeting her. I tell her I love you…..she smiles, I won't tell you the rest but us, we are planning for our marriage soon.

Participant 9

Participant 9 is a 31-year-old male who was captured from a wealthy Dinka family to become a child soldier. He managed to reunite with his family, who came to the U.S. after the war but went back to Sudan when peace returned. He is married, a Christian, and struggling to care for his family due to unemployment. At the time of the interview, he was planning to pursue higher education in order to offer a better life to his family.

Q1: How was your life prior to the Sudan conflict?

We had a good lifestyle, we had everything we needed, food, shelter and good clothes. Some families looked to us to give them food. My siblings attended the best schools in Juba. We were respected in our neighbourhood and many people loved us.

Q2: Tell me how the conflict transformed your life

Unfortunately, I developed a very ruthless heart towards people because of the suffering I was subjected to. As such am no longer friendly and am in most cases on my own as opposed to my earlier days. My health is poor due to change of climate and extreme weather. I walk with a limp as a result of a bullet in my right leg

Q3: How did it feel to be a soldier in your childhood age, if you were one? How did you become a soldier?

On that fateful evening, we were playing with my friends as we left from school. It was a hot afternoon and we were in great moods. Unfortunately, they beat us and put us in their tracks. Being a child soldier ruined al my dreams and I felt very desperate as I served in the camps

Q4: Tell me about the suffering and physical abuse, if any, you experienced during the conflict. How did that happen?

One day, they shot me in my right leg because I had refused to participate in killing the rest of my Sudanese friends who were not soldiers. They brought some doctors to treat me as they watched over me. I kept thinking they were going to kill me but they did not. It was so painful and even to date I still walk with a limp.

Q5: Describe any violence you witnessed during the conflict. What was your reaction?

They shot my friends as I watched. Worse still, they made me shoot my uncle on the head. It was one of the most traumatizing events of my lifetime. I screamed with hysteria but the militia beat me up to silence me. This unfortunately cased me to have no human heart.

Q 6.Tell me of any physical displacement you suffered?

I was displaced within Sudan for three times. I was subjected to wild animals, lack of food and water. I remember one particular day that we had to swim a treacherous river and many of my friends drowned.

What did you do after that happened?

I was exposed to mutilated and dead bodies. The most traumatizing incidence was when I had to leave behind my elder sister about to die. She was so sick, there was no hope for her, and we had to flee from the militia.

Q 7. How did you leave Sudan?

We walked as a group for many days. We were subjected to wild animals and hunger in the wilderness. It was one of the worst experiences of my life. One day, my friend was attacked by a large snake that swallowed her alive. We watched helplessly from a distance. This was one of my worst experiences of my lifetime. After many days we entered to Kenya and camped at a camp known as Kakuma

How did you get to the US?

The UNHCR (United Nations High Commission for Refugees) relocated us as a group one evening from Kakuma refugee camp in Kenya

What was the experience?

The UNHCR had relocated a large number of us, which slowed down the settlement process. We suffered a great deal since we were exposed to harsh weather and fatigue. Due to diverse cultural and religion differences, it was very hard to cope with the my new environment.

Q 8. What are the mental or physical challenges, if any, you have faced since you left Sudan?

I keep having depression due to the memory of the people who died as I watched especially my uncle, the multiples of lifeless bodies that lay on the ground, not to mention of the widespread burnings. Even as I write, I can still see them in my mind. When I first arrived, I felt that my life had come to an end; the wind chill made it seem like 5 degrees. I had never seen snow in my life; I could not seem to adapt. Three months later, I was attacked by a group of five youths while I was waiting for the bus at 11 o'clock. One demanded that I go to the ATM and withdraw all the money I had. I told them I was a newcomer and I had no money. On hearing that, one of them jumped me, and hit me on the head; the others also attacked me and stole my jacket, pants, shoes, and bus pass. I was freezing. Finally, the ambulance came and I was taken to the hospital . . . . Low income and having enough to eat were also difficult. Telephone bills, rent, hydro, food, etc. on $370.00 a month is not enough. Sometimes I would go to my friend's house for dinner. I went to see my counselor at Welcome Place and he tried to help me. In the end, he said that I would have to learn to survive on that income. As a result of my situation, I quit school and looked for a job. Lucky for me, I found a job with a tire company. I can get by better financially".

How did it feel?

I was so bitter and frightened, even to date, I am easily startled. Sometimes I feel like I would beat to somebody just because he or she said hi to me. These are the days that I am bitter. Sometimes I feel so lonely with so much emotion drain

Q 9. How did your sufferings affect your interactions with others and your perception of other communities in Sudan and in South Dakota?

With my Christian grounds, I keep trying to like them even though it is still a long journey, as I have not healed emotionally. However, I have made a few friends from the different communities since they have been nice to me.

Q 10. How does it feel living in the US as compared to living in Sudan? Please explain

Living in the US is better as compared to Sudan and it makes me feel a little more respected since the militia is not here to traumatize us again. However, being jobless, the economic status is almost unbearable. You cannot imagine the bills that I have to pay every end of the month

Q11: Tell me of any psychological treatment you have received so far here in the US?

I was treated for PTSD (Post-traumatic stress order) due to the frequent nightmares and depression I had

Q 12. What was your religion prior to the war and was it one of the factors that caused your suffering and displacement in Sudan?

I was a Christian protestant. It did not really contribute to the sufferings and displacements since Christianity was the only region that was recognized in Sudan. It is an advantage to be a Christian since you are not discriminated from the rest. Besides, being a Christian is one of the best things that happened to me

What is your opinion on other religions in South Dakota?

I personally had any negative opinion to our fellow Catholics and Muslims. I considered them as my friends despite the diverse differences we shared

Q 13. Have you been able to get new friends in South Dakota and how have you been affected in terms of emotional drain that resulted from losing your friends?

I have very few friends in South Dakota. It is hard for me to make new friends and keep them due to the emotion drain that I went through

Q 14. How have you changed in terms of handling anger and other emotional feelings? Has the counseling been of any help?

I must admit that the counseling has been helpful. With time, I am able to laugh and smile at people. This has taken long though. The nightmares reduce by the day. The other day, somebody hit me from behind by mistake. This made me drop my bag and I almost fell down. He apologized. At first, I was very offended and ready to defend myself but after he apologized, to my surprise, my anger vanished. As matter of truth, if it were the earlier days, I would have hurled insults at him if not jumping on him to attack him!

Q 15. How have you related with those people who are natives in South Dakota? Do you share issues of life with them or do you share with your colleagues from Sudan?

I am able to relate with the natives in South Dakota as time goes by but my main challenge is the culture, ethnic differences between us. It was difficult in the beginning but it has improved as days goes by. I prefer sharing my issues of life with my colleagues from Sudan

Q 16. What was your family life like prior to the war?

My family at Juba was the best as I can recall. We all loved each other and had everything we ever needed. My parents and siblings were all alive and healthy

Q17. What was your family life like after the war?

My sister died during the war it remains one of my worst nightmares. My parents were separated and the rest of my siblings lived on their own

Q18. How is your family life now?

We have been reunited with my parents and siblings. You cannot imagine of how happy we are with my siblings and parent s. It has been a wonderful experience. The best thing is that I am now married but due to the economic hardships, we are yet to get children. My marriage and family has given me reason to live by the day.

Participant 10

Participant 10 is a 35-year-old female who was captured by the militia and forced to take care of the soldiers at the camp. She was working in a security firm at the time of the interview. Her foster parents managed to educate her, and this helped her to find a well paying job in the U.S. She was a Muslim before the war broke, but she converted to Christianity while in the U.S. She is from the Dinka tribe in Sudan.

Q1: How was your life prior to the Sudan conflict?

I attended school and sometimes had to take break to attend to my father's cattle. Food was not a major challenge and we also had good clothes. We attended madrasa classes and I loved my Muslim friends and Christian friends

Q2: Tell me how the conflict transformed your life

One of my brothers joined a militia group as a soldier at the age of 14 while my Dad was killed. We fled with my mother and three siblings. We stayed in the forest eating wild fruits for two weeks as we walked for long distances. One of my siblings died of hunger and we were lucky to reach at Kakuma Refugee camp in Kenya after three months. Our education was interrupted and we did not attend school in the refugee camp where we stayed for 13 months until we relocated to South Dakota with the help of UNHCR

Q3: How did it feel to be a soldier in your childhood age, if you were one? How did you become a soldier?

I joined the militia forcibly when I was kidnapped from home and taken to the forest where the militia was training children and youths. My two other friends who we got to know each other while in the militia group were kidnapped from school. We cooked for the militia group, washed their clothes and we were used to spy the areas of attack. The girls were used as wives by the soldiers and those who failed to comply were threatened to death or killed. We were taken through rituals and given oath to remain in the group. We could watch the militia men kill our friends and relatives and this has ever filled us with guilt and pain.

Q4: Tell me about the suffering and physical abuse, if any, you experienced during the conflict. How did that happen?

We walked for long distances as we looked for water and food, often we could watch our kids die of hunger and thirst while our friends and relatives were attacked by wild animals, some were drowned and others died of snake bites in the forest.

Q5: Describe any violence you witnessed during the conflict. What was your reaction?

Some of our friends were killed; there was widespread burning, looting and shelling. I was raped countless times by the male colleagues we were with during our travel from Sudan to Kakuma Refugee camp. My own children were also raped and I could not protect them.

Q6: Tell me of any physical displacement you suffered?

At the break of War, were internally displaced as several families, we left our homes to hide in schools and in police camps. When the militia groups and armed forces started raiding schools and police camps we were again displaced again.

What did you do after that happened?

We agreed as huge groups of the internally displaced people to leave Sudan for Kakuma Refugee Camp in Kenya. We had to find our way out of the country by walking for long distances where we were highly insecure.

Q7: How did you leave Sudan?

I escaped from the camp one day during a fight against our enemies. They had attacked us in one of our camps and we had to flee. I hid in the forest and kept walking until I caught up with a group of people that were walking through the forest towards Kenya. We took about three months to get to Kakuma Refugee Camp through walking from Sudan.

How did you get to the US?

While at the refugee camp, we were lucky to be listed in the UNHCR list of those who would be relocated to United States and that is how I managed to arrive at South Dakota.

What was the experience?

I faced various traumatic events including killings, starving, kidnapping and faced harsh conditions. However at Kakuma, there was peace though we hardly got enough food. We were given one meal in six days.

Q8: What are the mental or physical challenges, if any, you have faced since you left Sudan?

It took me six months to re-unite with my mother and 8 months to re-unite with my siblings. During this time I used to have nightmares, I would often scream at night. I hated my situation and I was always stressed. In the camp we starved, had no clothes and most families fought at night over meals. Life however changed upon arriving at South Dakota, we could at least have a meal for each day and my sibling got a job that enabled us to feed and at least get clothes.

How did it feel?

It was relieving to arrive at Kakuma since in the camp we had peace. However we often starved since the relief aid agencies could not feed us all. Arriving at South Dakota was a safe haven for us, though we still struggled to start life afresh, we at least managed to get enough food and people would get jobs that helped us to live well.

Q9: How does it feel living in the US as compared to living in Sudan? Please explain

There is peace in the new home country and this gives hope for our future since the kids are able to go to school. The country has job opportunities and those with education can secure jobs. The challenge is that house rent, hospital and food bills are very high. Underemployment and unemployment are the major challenges. However those with education are sometimes humiliated working at very low profile jobs. Such people in Sudan would secure good jobs especially those who have degrees in education and medicine or nursing. These degrees are hardly recognized in the new home country and Sudanese often go for low profile jobs like security guards.

Q10: Tell me of any psychological treatment you have received so far here in the US?

Community development groups and UN agencies like UNHCR has been giving us counselling and this has so much helped us to deal with our past. This has enabled us to deal with our past that has been full of traumatic events, the counselling has enabled us to realize that we have a future and our lives can be better.

Q11: Tell me of any psychological treatment you have received so far here in the US?

Community development groups and UN agencies like UNHCR has been giving us counselling and this has so much helped us to deal with our past. This has enabled us to deal with our past that has been full of traumatic events, the counseling has enabled us to realize that we have a future and our lives can be better.

Q 12. What was your religion prior to the war and was it one of the factors that caused your suffering and displacement in Sudan?

Before we left Sudan, I was a Muslim and we lived in Northern Sudan. Northern Sudan was dominated by Islamic community and Christians were very few. I had no Christian friends. When war broke, I fled to the forest and in the forest, we were mixed with southerners who were mainly Christians. For this reason, I could be discriminated particularly in the centres for displaced people where sometimes those of us who were Muslims were made to go without food and other necessities that were donated by humanitarian organizations. After long-suffering in Kakuma, I decided to join the Christian community and after sometime, I was converted to Christianity, which made life a little easier. In South Dakota, Christianity was predominant and most of my Muslim friends converted to Christians since there were even no facilities like Mosque or Quran.

Q 13. Have you been able to get new friends in South Dakota and how have you been affected in terms of emotional drain that resulted from losing your friends?
For some time I only remained with my Sudanese friends and I feared interacting with the Dakota natives since our cultures are very different and I often did not fit in their talks and activities. However, after getting a job with a security company, I have managed to make friends from my work colleagues and also in my neighborhood. I keep remembering my friends some of who lost during the war and others I left them in the camp. However, counseling has enabled me handle my emotions in a better way and at least I have found new friends from my Sudanese community and from Dakota.

Q 14. How have you changed in terms of handling anger and other emotional feelings? Has the counseling been of any help?
While in the camp, I often fought with my colleagues over small issues including food and other basics. I also got mistreated by my seniors and thus resolved to mistreat my juniors also. Sometimes out of anger, I attempted suicide severally but got rescued by my colleagues. It is during one of those attempts that I was identified by one of the workers with the aid agencies who recommended me for counseling. Counseling has so much changed my views and my reaction to other people's actions. It has particularly helped me to deal with anger in a better way.

Q 15. A. How have you related with those people who are natives in South Dakota?
I only share with those people who we work with, more often we share issues to do with work and not family and other issues since we have very little in common. I often feel miserable when we share about things like education advancement, families and other areas, which I feel I have lost.

B. Do you share issues of life with them or do you share with your colleagues from Sudan?
I hardly share my life issues with Dakota natives; mainly due to fear of how they will take them and also due to cultural differences that has shaped our views differently. In our Sudanese community, a woman cannot call a man a fool but in the American community, it is not hard to hear such things and this instills fear in most of us particularly men who do not want to feel dishonored in terms of gender. Some of the issues where our culture differs include how issues like family conflicts and dissolutions are handled and how we were used to address such issues in our Sudanese culture where men were highly respected and often remained decision makers. Women and children are highly protected in South Dakota and a small issue can raise a legal concern. For this reason, I avoid sharing many issues with people of Dakota since they may think am primitive. May be acculturation will help me in the future to fully understand them and thus be open in my thinking and my views with them.

Q 16. What was your family life like prior to the war?

Before the break of the war, we lived in Southern Sudan with our family including my mother, father and four siblings. We attended school and had no struggle accessing necessities like food shelter, health and education.

Q17. What was your family life like after the war?

During the war, my father was killed, my mother fled with 2 of my sisters and we did not manage to reconnect after the war. My two brothers and I managed to arrive at Kakuma Refugee in Kenya but one of my brothers died while in the refugee camp. I got an opportunity for relocation to South Dakota but my brother was left at Kakuma.

Q18. How is your family life now?

Today I have no connection with any of my family members and it is one of the most stressful thing in my life since I keep thinking about my mother and always wonder whether she is alive together with my sisters or not. I plan to marry may be after I have fully settled in my job and I would prefer to marry from my Sudanese community since I'm familiar with them. I don't think I have hopes of finding my family members.

ELIAS RINALDO GAMBORIKO, AJ. PH.D, Ed. D.

Elias Rinaldo Gamboriko, AJ. Ph.D

SUMMARY OF QUALIFICATIONS

Visionary Counselor and Teacher offering 15+ years of creative, compelling style that has proven to be inspirational and successful. Versatile executive strategist recognized for having superior leadership skills, exceptional mentorship abilities, and superlative teaching acumen. Progressive and caring individual, highly valued for expertise in personal growth, translating objectives into actionable plans, and providing decisive leadership to multi-functional staff. Currently seeking a position which will effectively utilize all acquired skills, abilities, and areas of expertise as follows:

☐ Spiritual Growth Leadership	☐ Mentorship & Teaching	☐ Personnel Development
☐ Ministering Holy Sacraments.	☐ Relationship Building	☐ Team Leadership
☐ Project Management	☐ Sermon Preparation/Delivery	☐ Strategic Planning
☐ Congregational Strategy	☐ Logistical Coordination	☐ Conflict Resolution
☐ Prayer Development	☐ Marketing/Advertising	☐ Ethics & Integrity
☐ Operations Management		

EDUCATION HISTORY

Argosy University, Phoenix, AZ | Doctor of Psychology (Ph. D) Ed. D. in Pastoral Community Counseling Psychology Major (Dec. 2012). USA.
Aberdeen University, Idaho | Doctor of Philosophy & Theology, Ph.D. (Nov. 2007). USA.
Creighton Jesuit University, Omaha, NE | M.A. in Christian Spirituality & Counseling Psychology (Jun. 2006). USA.
Pontifical Urbaniana University, Rome, Italy | B.A. in Theology & Philosophy (May 1999)

CERTIFICATIONS

- ♦ National Association of Catholic Chaplains | Certified Chaplain (NACC).
- ♦ Member of the American Psychological Association (APA).
- ♦ Ordained to Priesthood in Tombura-Yambio Catholic Diocese South Sudan
- ♦ Apostles of Jesus Youth Technical Institute | Certification
- ♦ National Trade Test Certificate Grad 111, Nairobia, Kenya
- ♦ Sudan Intermediate Leaving Certificate, South Sudan, Africa
- ♦ Sudan Primary Leaving Certificate, South Sudan, Africa
- ♦ CPE Training. Association for Clinical Pastoral Education
- ♦ Attended a courses in Trauma and Recovery- Kenya Africa

PROFESSIONAL PROFILE

Full-Time Assistant Professor of Chung-Jen College. Republic of China-Taiwan-Asia.	*2014*
Catholic Diocese of Alexandria Louisiana-USA. *Assistant Pastor.*	*2013–2014*
Catholic Diocese of Sioux Falls · *Chaplain*	2004-2013

Catholic Diocese of Sioux Falls/St. Lombard Catholic School · *Advisor & Teacher* 2008-2013
Catholic Diocese of Sioux Falls/St. Josephine Bakhita Catholic Parish · *Pastor* 2004-2013
Catholic Diocese of Rumbek/St. Josephine Formation Center · *Rector & Teacher* 2000-2003
Catholic Diocese of Rumbek/Kakuma Refugees Camp Kenya · *Assistant Pastor* 1999
Catholic Diocese of Alexandria Louisiana-USA

<u>**PRESENTATIONS**</u>
- Ph. D Candidate (Nov. 15th, 2012) - A phenomenological study of the lost generation of Sudan / Dissertation defense / Argosy University / Sioux Falls, South Dakota.

<u>PROFESSIONAL AFFILIATIONS</u>

- Catholic Priest of the Apostles of Jesus – January 13th, 1999
- Member of the Apostles of Jesus Missionaries for Africa and the world – 1980
- Attended a courses in Trauma and Recovery- Kenya Africa 20002
- Rector/teacher St. Josephine Bakhita Formation Center- Kitale-Kenya – 200-2003
- CPE Training. Association for Clinical Pastoral Education 2004. USA
- A certified Chaplain: Certified by The National Association of Catholic Chaplains (NACC) - USA in 2006 and renewed in 2011.
- Teacher & Advisor St. Lombard Catholic School Sioux Falls Catholic Diocese- 2005-2013
- Chaplain Avera Mckennan Hospital Sioux Falls, South Dakota USA 2004-2013
- Member of the American Psychological Association (APA) - 2013
- Pastor of St. Josephine Bakhita Parish/assistant – St Joseph Cathedral / Sioux Falls-2004
- Chaplain Avera Behavioral Hospital Sioux Falls- 2004 - 2008
- On Call Chaplain /Veteran Association (VA) Hospital Sioux Falls-2005-2013
- Parochial Vicar (September 10th, 2013) – St. Anthony of Padua Catholic Church-Alexandria Catholic Diocese-Louisiana.
- Full-Time Assistant Professor @ Chung-Jen College (February 1,2014) Republic of China – Taiwan -Asia.

<u>ACADEMIC AWARDS</u>

Title of Award	Granting Institution	Dates
☐ Faculty Excellence in Teaching	Chung-Jen College of Nursing, Health Sciences and Management. Dalin Township Taiwan-Republic of China.	March 10, 20414
♦ Faculty Excellence of Speech Presentation on Tourism, Environment & Culture.	Trans World University Douliu City Taiwan. Republic of China.	March 28, 2014
♦ Attended Course on Water Resources, Ecology and Environment	Taiwan Water Recourses, Ecology, Forestry and Environmental Department.	June 26, 2014

VOLUNTEER EXPERIENCE

- Catholic Chaplain Chung-Jen College (February 1,2014) Republic of China – Taiwan -Asia.
- Pastor (2004 – 2013) - Catholic Diocese of Sioux Falls / St. Joseph Cathedral Parish and St. Josephine Bakhita Catholic Parish / Sioux Falls, South Dakota
- President (2010 – 2013) - Sudan Missionary Initiative Inc. / President of Sudan Missionary Inc./ Sioux Falls, South Dakota-USA
- Parochial Vicar (September 10th, 2013) – St. Anthony of Padua Catholic Church-Alexandria Catholic Diocese-Louisiana.
- Full-Time Assistant Professor of Chung-Jen College (February 1,2014) Republic of China – Taiwan -Asia.

ADDITIONAL INFORMATION

Interests:

- Playing Soccer, Jogging, and workout in gymnasium, biking, reading books, research, Executive Chef and writing books

Books Written:

- The Psychological Effects of Multiple Roles in Priesthood and Religious life 2011
- Psychological Trauma and Post Traumatic Disorders / Soldiers (Child). 2010
- The Funny Risen Jesus. Elias Christology Now! 2011/2012